Fodor's 97 Pocket Washington, D.C.

D1487982

Reprinted from Fodor's *Washington, D.C.* '97

Fodor's Travel Publications, Inc.
New York • Toronto • London • Sydney • Auckland
http://www.fodors.com/

Fodor's Pocket Washington, D.C.

Editors: Neil Chesanow, Audra Epstein
Contributors: Rob Andrews, Holly Bass, Bob Blake, Anna Borgman, Mary Case, Michael Dolan, John F. Kelly, Deborah Papier, Jennifer Paull, Betty Ross, Nancy Ryder, Linda K. Schmidt, Mary Ellen Schultz, Dinah Spritzer, M. T. Schwartzman, Bruce Walker, Jan Ziegler
Creative Director: Fabrizio La Rocca
Cartographer: David Lindroth
Cover Photograph: Doug Armand/TSW
Text Design: Between the Covers

Copyright

Special Sales

Fodor's Travel Publications are available at special discounts for bulk purchases for sales promotions or premiums. Special editions, including personalized covers, excerpts of existing guides, and corporate imprints, can be created in large quantities for special needs. For more information, contact your local bookseller or write to Special Markets, Fodor's Travel Publications, 201 East 50th Street, New York, NY 10022. Inquiries from Canada should be directed to your local Canadian bookseller or sent to Random House of Canada, Ltd., Marketing Department, 1265 Aerowood Drive, Mississauga, Ontario L4W 1B9. Inquiries from the United Kingdom should be sent to Fodor's Travel Publications, 20 Vauxhall Bridge Road, London SW1V 2SA.

PRINTED IN THE UNITED STATES OF AMERICA

10 9 8 7 6 5 4 3 2 1

CONTENTS

On the Road with Fodor's   v

On the Web *v*
New and Noteworthy *v*
How to Use This Book *vi*
Don't Forget to Write *vii*

Essential Information   *xii*

Important Contacts *xiii*
Smart Travel Tips *xxi*

1   Destination: Washington, D.C.   1

America's Hometown *2*
History at a Glance *4*
Presidents *5*

2   Exploring Washington   7

The Mall *9*
The Monuments *22*
The White House Area *28*
Capitol Hill *39*
Old Downtown and Federal Triangle *50*
Georgetown *58*
Dupont Circle *64*
Foggy Bottom *71*
Alexandria *74*
Around Washington *80*

3   Dining   85

4   Lodging   106

5   Nightlife and the Arts   120

6   Shopping   135

**   Index   151**

Maps

Washington, D.C., Area
viii–ix
Washington, D.C., Metro
  System *x–xi*
Exploring Washington,
  D.C. *10–11*
The Mall *14–15*
The Monuments *25*
The White House Area *30*
Capitol Hill *41*
Old Downtown and
  Federal Triangle *54–55*

Georgetown *61*
Dupont Circle and Foggy
  Bottom *66*
Old Town Alexandria *76*
Washington Dining *90–91*
Washington Lodging
110–111
Washington Shopping
138–139
Georgetown Shopping *141*

ON THE ROAD WITH FODOR'S

WE'RE ALWAYS thrilled to get letters from readers, especially one like this:

It took us an hour to decide what book to buy and we now know we picked the best one. Your book was wonderful, easy to follow, very accurate, and good on pointing out eating places, informal as well as formal. When we saw other people using your book, we would look at each other and smile.

Our editors and writers are deeply committed to making every Fodor's guide "the best one"— not only accurate but always charming, brimming with sound recommendations and solid ideas, right on the mark in describing restaurants and hotels, and full of fascinating facts that make you view what you've traveled to see in a rich new light.

On the Web

Also check out Fodor's Web site (http://www.fodors.com/), where you'll find travel information on major destinations around the world and an ever-changing array of travel-savvy interactive features.

New and Noteworthy

Smithsonian museums are trying to outdo one another this year: the **National Museum of African Art** and the **Arthur M. Sackler Gallery** team to present "Dar-Al-Islam: Art, Life and Cultures of the Islamic World" (late Apr.–late Oct.); "Cosmic Voyage," a new IMAX film, can be seen at the **National Air and Space Museum;** the newly refurbished gem hall has reopened at the **National Museum of Natural History;** and the **National Portrait Gallery** will have two rebel-themed exhibits: "East Coast/West Coast: Poet Rebels of the 1950s" (late Jan.–early May) and "Rebel Painters: The New York School, 1945–1960" (late Jan.–early June).

The **Phillips Collection** celebrates its most famous painting, Renoir's *Luncheon of the Boating Party,* with an exhibit of Impressionist artists such as Monet, Manet, and Pissaro (late Sept.–early Feb. 1997).

As for politics, last year was a year of big change on both the national and the local levels. The national electorate threw out the Democratic rascals in favor of Republican rascals. Former mayor Marion S. Barry Jr., voted out of office four years ago after a widely publicized drug sting landed him in jail, made an amazing comeback and was re-elected mayor of Washington. It happened just as the city's financial troubles were prompting talk in Congress of returning control of the city to the federal government. Ah, Washington . . .

How to Use This Book

Organization

Up front is **Essential Information.** Its first section, **Important Contacts,** gives addresses and telephone numbers of organizations and companies that offer destination-related services and detailed information and publications. **Smart Travel Tips,** the Gold Guide's second section, gives specific information on how to accomplish what you need to in Washington, D.C., as well as tips on savvy traveling. Both sections are in alphabetical order by topic.

The Exploring chapter is subdivided by neighborhood with sights listed alphabetically. The chapters that follow are arranged in alphabetical order by subject (dining, lodging, nightlife and the arts, and shopping.

Icons and Symbols

★ Our special recommendations
✕ Restaurant
🏨 Lodging establishment

🐤 Good for kids (rubber duckie)
☞ Sends you to another section of the guide for more information
⊠ Address
☎ Telephone number
FAX Fax number
🕐 Opening and closing times
💰 Admission prices (those we give apply only to adults; substantially reduced fees are almost always available for children, students, and senior citizens)

Hotel Facilities

We always list the facilities that are available—but we don't specify whether they cost extra: When pricing accommodations, always ask what's included.

Restaurant Reservations and Dress Codes

Reservations are always a good idea; we note only when they're essential or when they are not accepted. Book as far ahead as you can, and reconfirm when you get to town. Unless otherwise noted, the restaurants listed are open daily for lunch and dinner. We mention dress only when men are required to wear a jacket or a jacket and tie.

Credit Cards

The following abbreviations are used: **AE,** American Express; **D,** Discover; **DC,** Diners Club; **MC,** MasterCard; and **V,** Visa.

Don't Forget to Write

You can use this book in the confidence that all prices and opening times are based on information supplied to us at press time; Fodor's cannot accept responsibility for any errors. Time inevitably brings changes, so always confirm information when it matters—especially if you're making a detour to visit a specific place. In addition, when making reservations be sure to mention if you have a disability or are traveling with children, if you prefer a private bath or a certain type of bed, or if you have specific dietary needs or any other concerns.

Were the restaurants we recommended as described? Did our hotel picks exceed your expectations? Did you find a museum we recommended a waste of time? If you have complaints, we'll look into them and revise our entries when the facts warrant it. If you've discovered a special place that we haven't included, we'll pass the information along to our correspondents and have them check it out. So send your feedback, positive *and* negative, to the Washington, D.C., editor at 201 East 50th Street, New York, New York 10022—and have a wonderful trip!

Karen Cure
Editorial Director

Washington, D.C. Area

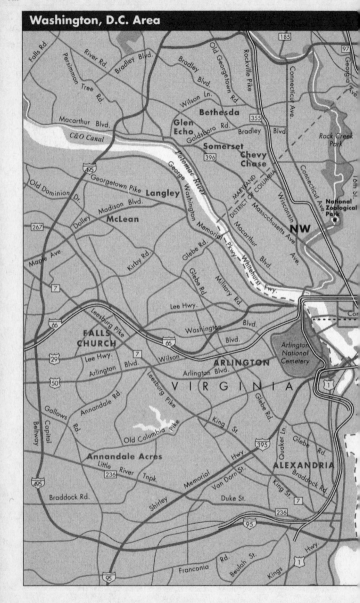

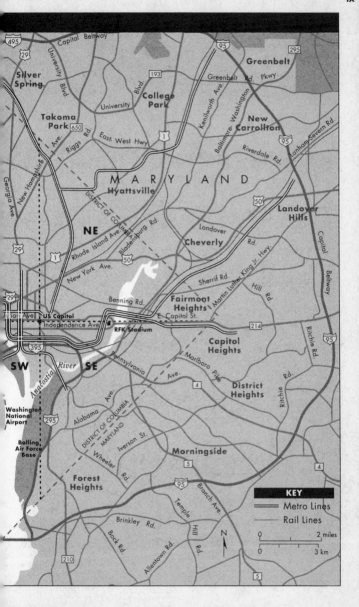

KEY

Metro Lines
Rail Lines

N

| 0 | | 2 miles |
| 0 | | 3 km |

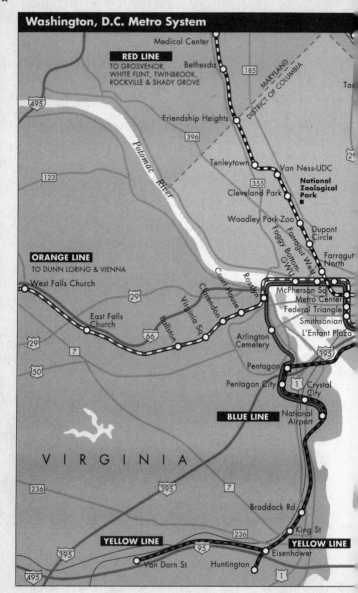

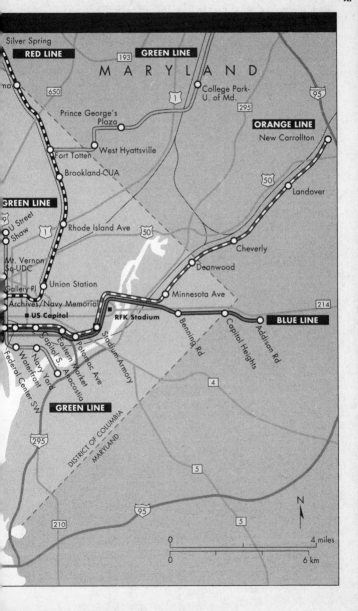

Essential
Information

IMPORTANT CONTACTS

An Alphabetical Listing of Publications, Organizations, and Companies that Will Help You Before, During, and After Your Trip

AIR TRAVEL

The major gateways to Washington, D.C., include **National Airport** (☎ 703/419–8000), in Virginia, 4 miles south of downtown Washington; **Dulles International Airport** (☎ 703/661–2700), 26 miles west of Washington; and **Baltimore-Washington International (BWI) Airport** (☎ 410/859–7100), in Maryland, about 25 miles northeast of Washington.

CARRIERS

TO NATIONAL AIRPORT➤ Contact **Air Canada** (☎ 800/776–3000), **America West** (☎ 800/235–9292), **American Airlines** (☎ 800/433–7300), **Continental** (☎ 800/525–0280), **Delta** (☎ 800/221–1212), **Midway** (☎ 800/446–4392, **Northwest** (☎ 800/225–2525) **TWA** (☎ 800/221–2000), **United** (☎ 800/241–6522), and **USAir** (☎ 800/428–4322).

TO DULLES➤ Contact **Air Canada** (☎ 800/776–3000), **American Airlines** (☎ 800/433–7300), **Continental** (☎ 800/525–0280), **Delta** (☎ 800/221–1212), **Northwest** (☎ 800/225–2525), **TWA** (☎ 800/221–2000), **United** (☎ 800/241–6522), and **USAir** (☎ 800/428–

4322), and **Western Pacific** (☎ 800/930–3030.

TO BWI➤ Contact **America West** (☎ 800/235–9292), **American Airlines** (☎ 800/433–7300), **Continental** (☎ 800/525–0280), **Delta** (☎ 800/221–1212), **Northwest** (☎ 800/225–2525), **Southwest** (☎ 800/435–9792), **TWA** (☎ 800/221–2000), **United** (☎ 800/241–6522), and **USAir** (☎ 800/428–4322).

For inexpensive, no-frills flights, contact **MarkAir** (☎ 800/627–5247), **Midwest Express** (☎ 800/452–2022), **Prestige Airlines** (☎ 800/299–8784), **Private Jet** (☎ 404/231–7571, 800/546–7571, or 800/949–9400), and **ValuJet** (☎ 404/994–8258 or 800/825-8538).

AIRPORT TRANSFERS

BY BUS

National and Dulles airports are served continuously by **Washington Flyer** (☎ 703/685–1400). The ride from National to downtown takes 20 minutes and costs $8 ($14 round-trip); from Dulles, the 45-minute ride costs $16 ($26 round-trip). The bus takes you to 1517 K Street NW, where you can board a free shuttle bus that serves downtown hotels. The shuttle bus will also transport you from your hotel to the K Street address to catch the main airport bus on your return journey. Washington Flyer also provides service to Maryland and Virginia suburbs. Fares may be paid in cash or with Visa or MasterCard; children under age six ride free.

BWI SuperShuttle buses (☎ 800/ 809–7080) leave BWI every hour for 1517 K Street NW. The 65-minute ride costs $15 ($25 round-trip); drivers accept traveler's checks and major credit cards in addition to cash.

BY LIMOUSINE

Call at least a day ahead and **Diplomat Limousine** (☎ 703/461– 6800) will have a limousine waiting for you at the airport. The ride downtown from National or Dulles is about $75; it's $90 from BWI. **Private Car** (☎ 800/685– 0888) has a counter at BWI Airport and charges $63 from there to downtown; or call ahead to have a car waiting for you at National ($45) or Dulles ($73).

BY SUBWAY

A Metro station is within walking distance of the baggage claim area at Washington National Airport; a free airport shuttle stops outside each terminal and brings you to the National Airport station. The Metro ride downtown takes about 20 minutes and costs either $1.10

or $1.40, depending on the time of day.

BY TAXI

Expect to pay about $13 to get from National Airport to downtown, $45 from Dulles, and $50 from BWI. Unscrupulous cabbies prey on out-of-towners, so if the fare strikes you as astronomical, get the driver's name and cab number and threaten to call the **D.C. Taxicab Commission** (☎ 202/ 645–6018). A $1.25 airport surcharge is added to the total at National.

BY TRAIN

Free shuttle buses carry passengers between airline terminals and the train station at BWI Airport. **Amtrak** (☎ 800/872–7245) and **Maryland Rail Commuter Service** (MARC, ☎ 800/325–7245) trains run between BWI and Washington's Union Station from around 6 AM to midnight. The cost of the 40-minute ride is $10 on an Amtrak train, $4.50 on a MARC train (weekdays only).

BUS TRAVEL

Washington is a major terminal for **Greyhound Bus Lines** (✉ 1005 1st St. NE, ☎ 202/289–5160 or 800/231–2222). Check with your local Greyhound ticket office for prices and schedules.

WITHIN WASHINGTON

For schedule and route information, contact the **Washington Metropolitan Area Transit Author-**

ity (WMATA, ☎ 202/637–7000, TTY 202/638–3780; open daily 6 AM–11:30 PM).

CAR RENTAL

The major car-rental companies represented in Washington, D.C., are **Alamo** (☎ 800/327–9633; in the U.K., 0800/272–2000), **Avis** (☎ 800/331–1212; in Canada, 800/879–2847), **Budget** (☎ 800/527–0700; in the U.K., 0800/181181), **Dollar** (☎ 800/800–4000; in the U.K., 0990/565656, where it is known as Eurodollar), **Hertz** (☎ 800/654–3131; in Canada, 800/263–0600; in the U.K., 0345/555888), and **National InterRent** (☎ 800/227–7368; in the U.K., where National is known as Europcar InterRent, 0345/222525). Rates in Washington begin at $40 a day and $149 a week for an economy car with unlimited mileage. This does not include tax on car rentals, which is 8%.

RENTAL WHOLESALERS
Contact **Auto Europe** (☎ 207/828–2525 or 800/223–5555).

DISABILITIES & ACCESSIBILITY

ORGANIZATIONS
TRAVELERS WITH HEARING IMPAIR-MENTS➤ The **American Academy of Otolaryngology** (⊠ 1 Prince St., Alexandria, VA 22314, ☎ 703/836–4444, FAX 703/683–5100, TTY 703/519–1585) publishes a brochure, "Travel Tips for Hearing Impaired People."

TRAVELERS WITH MOBILITY PROB-LEMS➤ Contact the **Information Center for Individuals with Disabilities** (⊠ Box 256, Boston, MA 02117, ☎ 617/450–9888; in MA, 800/462–5015; TTY 617/424–6855); **Mobility International USA** (⊠ Box 10767, Eugene, OR 97440, ☎ and TTY 541/343–1284, FAX 541/343–6812), the U.S. branch of a Belgium-based organization with affiliates in 30 countries; **MossRehab Hospital Travel Information Service** (☎ 215/456–9600, TTY 215/456–9602), a telephone information resource for travelers with physical disabilities; the **Society for the Advancement of Travel for the Handicapped** (⊠ 347 5th Ave., Suite 610, New York, NY 10016, ☎ 212/447–7284, FAX 212/725–8253; membership $45); and **Travelin' Talk** (⊠ Box 3534, Clarksville, TN 37043, ☎ 615/552–6670, FAX 615/552–1182) which provides local contacts worldwide for travelers with disabilities.

TRAVELERS WITH VISION IMPAIR-MENTS➤ Contact the **American Council of the Blind** (⊠ 1155 15th St. NW, Suite 720, Washington, DC 20005, ☎ 202/467–5081, FAX 202/467–5085) for a list of travelers' resources or the **American Foundation for the Blind** (⊠ 11 Penn Plaza, Suite 300, New York, NY 10001, ☎ 212/502–7600 or 800/232–5463, TTY 212/502–7662), which provides general advice and publishes "Access to Art" ($19.95), a directory of museums that accommodate travelers with vision impairments.

EMERGENCIES

Dial 911 for **police, fire,** or **ambulance** in an emergency.

DOCTOR

Prologue (☎ 202/362–8677) is a referral service that locates doctors, dentists, and urgent-care clinics in the greater Washington area. The hospital closest to downtown is **George Washington University Hospital** (901 23rd St. NW, ☎ 202/994–3211, emergencies only).

DENTIST

The **D.C. Dental Society** (☎ 202/547–7615) operates a referral line weekdays 8–4.

24-HOUR PHARMACY

CVS Pharmacy operates 24-hour pharmacies at 14th Street and Thomas Circle NW (☎ 202/628–0720) and at 7 Dupont Circle NW (☎ 202/785–1466).

GAY & LESBIAN TRAVEL

PUBLICATIONS

The premier international travel magazine for gays and lesbians is **Our World** (✉ 1104 N. Nova Rd., Suite 251, Daytona Beach, FL 32117, ☎ 904/441–5367, FAX 904/441–5604; $35 for 10 issues). The 16-page monthly **"Out & About"** (☎ 212/645–6922 or 800/929–2268, FAX 800/929–

2215; $49 for 10 issues and quarterly calendar) covers gay-friendly resorts, hotels, cruise lines, and airlines.

INSURANCE

IN CANADA

Contact **Mutual of Omaha** (✉ Travel Division, 500 University Ave., Toronto, Ontario M5G 1V8, ☎ 800/465–0267 (in Canada) or 416/598-4083).

IN THE U.S.

Travel insurance covering baggage, health, and trip cancellation or interruptions is available from **Access America** (✉ 6600 W. Broad St., Richmond, VA 23230, ☎ 804/285–3300 or 800/334–7525), **Carefree Travel Insurance** (✉ Box 9366, 100 Garden City Plaza, Garden City, NY 11530, ☎ 516/294–0220 or 800/323–3149), **Near Travel Services** (✉ Box 1339, Calumet City, IL 60409, ☎ 708/868–6700 or 800/654–6700), **Tele-Trip** (✉ Mutual of Omaha Plaza, Box 31716, Omaha, NE 68131, ☎ 800/228–9792), **Travel Guard International** (✉ 1145 Clark St., Stevens Point, WI 54481, ☎ 715/345–0505 or 800/826–1300), **Travel Insured International** (✉ Box 280568, East Hartford, CT 06128, ☎ 203/528–7663 or 800/243–3174), and **Wallach & Company** (✉ 107 W. Federal St., Box 480, Middleburg, VA 22117, ☎ 540/687–3166 or 800/237–6615).

IN THE U.K.

The **Association of British Insurers** (⊠ 51 Gresham St., London EC2V 7HQ, ☎ 0171/600–3333) gives advice by phone and publishes the free pamphlet **"Holiday Insurance and Motoring Abroad,"** which sets out typical policy provisions and costs.

LODGING

For a complete listing of hotels in the area, contact the Washington, D.C., Convention and Visitors Association (⊠ 1212 New York Ave. NW, Washington, DC 20005, ☎ 202/789–7000). **Capitol Reservations** books rooms at more than 70 better hotels in good locations at rates 20%–40% off (☎ 202/452–1270 or 800/847–4832 from 9 to 6 weekdays); the company also sells packages with tours and meals. **Washington D.C. Accommodations** will book rooms in any hotel in town, with discounts of 20%–40% at about 40 locations (☎ 202/289–2220 or 800/554–2220 from 9 to 5 weekdays).

MONEY

ATMS

For specific **Cirrus** locations in the United States and Canada, call 800/424–7787. For U.S. **Plus** locations, call 800/843–7587 and enter the area code and first three digits of the number from which you're calling (or of the calling area in which you want to locate an ATM).

PASSPORTS & VISAS

U.K. CITIZENS

For fees, documentation requirements, and to request an emergency passport, call the **London Passport Office** (☎ 0990/210410). For U.S. visa information, call the **U.S. Embassy Visa Information Line** (☎ 01891/200–290; calls cost 49p per minute or 39p per minute cheap rate) or send a self-addressed, stamped envelope to the **U.S. Embassy Visa Branch** (⊠ 5 Upper Grosvenor St., London W1A 2JB). If you live in Northern Ireland, write to the **U.S. Consulate General** (⊠ Queen's House, Queen St., Belfast BTI 6EO).

SENIOR CITIZENS

ORGANIZATIONS

Contact the **American Association of Retired Persons** (⊠ AARP, 601 E St. NW, Washington, DC 20049, ☎ 202/434–2277; annual dues $8 per person or couple). Its Purchase Privilege Program secures discounts for members on lodging, car rentals, and sightseeing, and the AARP Motoring Plan (☎ 800/334–3300) furnishes domestic trip-routing information and emergency road-service aid for an annual fee of $39.95 ($59.95 for a premium version). Senior citizen travelers can also join the AAA for emergency road service and other travel benefits.

Additional sources for discounts on lodgings, car rentals, and other travel expenses, as well as helpful magazines and newsletters, are the **National Council of Senior Citizens** (⊠ 1331 F St. NW, Washington, DC 20004, ☎ 202/347–8800; annual membership $12) and Sears's **Mature Outlook** (⊠ Box 10448, Des Moines, IA 50306, ☎ 800/336–6330; annual membership $14.95).

SIGHTSEEING

ORIENTATION TOURS

Tourmobile buses (☎ 202/554–7950 or 202/554–5100), authorized by the National Park Service, stop at 18 historic sights between the Capitol and Arlington National Cemetery; the route includes the White House and the museums on the Mall. Tickets are $10.

Old Town Trolley Tours (☎ 301/985–3021), orange-and-green motorized trolleys, take in the main downtown sights and also foray into Georgetown and the upper northwest, stopping at out-of-the-way attractions such as Washington National Cathedral. Tickets are $16.

BOAT TOURS

D.C. Ducks (⊠ 1323 Pennsylvania Ave. NW, ☎ 202/966–3825) offers 90-minute tours in their converted World War II amphibious vehicles. After an hour-long road tour of prominent sights, the tour moves from land to water, as the vehicle is piloted into the waters of the Potomac for a 30-minute boat's-eye view of the city. Tours run continuously from 10 AM to 4 PM from March through November. Tickets are $16.

The enclosed boat **The Dandy** (⊠ Prince St., between Duke and King Sts., Alexandria, VA, ☎ 703/683–6076 or 703/683–6090) cruises up the Potomac past the Lincoln Memorial to the Kennedy Center and Georgetown. Lunch cruises board weekdays starting at 10:30 AM and weekends starting at 11:30 AM. Dinner cruises board Monday–Thursday at 6 PM, Friday at 7:30 PM, and Sunday at 7:15 PM. A $21 "midnight cruise" boards at 11:30 PM April–October at Washington Harbour in Georgetown or in Alexandria. Prices are $26–$30 for lunch and $48–$56 for dinner.

The **Spirit of Washington** (⊠ Pier 4, 6th and Water Sts. SW, ☎ 202/554–8000), offers lunch cruises Tuesday–Saturday at 11:30 AM and a Sunday brunch cruise at 1. Evening cruises board at 6:30 PM and include dinner and a floor show. Adult "Moonlight Party" cruises board Friday and Saturday at 11:15 PM. Prices range from $21 per person for the moonlight cruise to $55 for dinner on Friday or Saturday night. A sister ship, the **Potomac Spirit,** sails to Mount Vernon, mid-March–October, Tuesday–Sunday. During peak tourist season (mid-June–August), boats depart at 9 AM and 2 PM.

From mid-March through mid-June and September through October, boats leave at 9 AM only. Tickets are $22.

BUS TOURS

All About Town, Inc. (✉ 519 6th St. NW, ☎ 202/393–3696) has half-day, all-day, two-day, and twilight bus tours that drive by some sights (e.g., memorials, museums, government buildings) and stop at others. Tours leave from the company's office at 7:45 AM March–September and at 8:15 AM October–February. An all-day tour costs $30.

Gray Line Tours (☎ 301/386–8300) has a four-hour tour of Washington, Embassy Row, and Arlington National Cemetery that leaves Union Station at 8:30 AM and 2 PM (at 2 PM only November–March; adults $22, children 3–11 $11); tours of Mount Vernon and Alexandria depart at 8:30 AM (adults $20, children $10). An all-day trip combining both tours leaves at 8:30 AM ($36).

SPECIAL-INTEREST TOURS

Special tours of government buildings—including the Archives, the Capitol, the FBI Building, the Supreme Court, and the White House—can be arranged through your representative's or senator's office. Limited numbers of these so-called VIP tickets are available, so plan up to six months in advance of your trip. With these special passes, your tour will often take you through rooms not normally open to the public.

WALKING TOURS

The **Black History National Recreation Trail** links a group of sights within historic neighborhoods illustrating aspects of African-American history in Washington, from slavery days to the New Deal. A brochure outlining the trail is available from the National Park Service (✉ 1100 Ohio Dr. SW, Washington, DC 20242, ☎ 202/619–7222).

The National Building Museum (☎ 202/272–2448) sponsors several architecture tours including the **"Construction Watch Tour"** ($7), which accompanies architects and construction-project managers to buildings in various stages of completion, and **"Site Seeing"** tours ($60 including bus transportation and a boxed lunch), which are led by architectural historians and visit various Washington neighborhoods and well-known monuments, public buildings, and houses.

The **D.C. Foot Tour** (✉ Box 9001, Alexandria, VA 22304, ☎ 703/461–7364) is a walking tour of major historic sites.

SUBWAY TRAVEL

For schedule and route information, contact the **Washington**

Metropolitan Area Transit Authority (WMATA; ☎ 202/637–7000, TTY 202/638–3780; open daily 6 AM–11:30 PM).

TAXIS

Two major companies serving the District are **Capitol Cab** (☎ 202/546–2400) and **Diamond Cab** (☎ 202/387–6200). *See* Taxis *in* Smart Travel Tips for information on rates.

TRAIN TRAVEL

More than 80 trains a day arrive at Washington, D.C.'s **Union Station** on Capitol Hill (⊠ 50 Massachusetts Ave. NE, ☎ 202/484–7540 or 800/872–7245). Also *see* Airport Transfers, *above*.

VISITOR INFORMATION

Contact the **Washington, D.C., Convention and Visitors Association** (⊠ 1212 New York Ave. NW, 6th floor, Washington, DC 20005, ☎ 202/789–7000, FAX 202/789–7037), the **D.C. Committee to Promote Washington** (⊠ 1212 New York Ave. NW, 2nd Floor, Washington, DC 20005, ☎ 800/422–8644), and the **National Park Service** (⊠ Office of Public Affairs, National Capital Region, 1100 Ohio Dr. SW, Washington,

DC 20242, ☎ 202/619–7222, FAX 202/619–7302).

National Park Service information kiosks on the Mall, near the White House, next to the Vietnam Veterans Memorial, and at several other locations throughout the city can provide helpful information. **Dial-A-Park** (☎ 202/619–7275) is a recording of events at Park Service attractions in and around Washington. **Dial-A-Museum** (☎ 202/357–2020) is a recording of exhibits and special offerings at Smithsonian Institution museums.

If you're planning to visit sites in the surrounding areas, contact the **Maryland Department of Economic and Employment/Tourism Development** (⊠ Office of Tourist Development, 217 E. Redwood St., 9th floor, Baltimore, MD 21202, ☎ 410/767–3400, FAX 410/333–6643) and the **Virginia Division of Tourism** (⊠ 901 East Byrd St., Richmond, VA 23219, ☎ 804/786–4484 or 804/847–4882, FAX 804/786–1919). The **Virginia-Maryland Travel Center** (⊠ 1629 K St. NW, ☎ 202/659–5523, FAX 202/659–8646) can book accommodations at Virginia B&Bs (☎ 800/934–9184).

SMART TRAVEL TIPS

Basic Information on Traveling in Washington and Savvy Tips to Make Your Trip a Breeze

AIR TRAVEL

If time is an issue, **always look for nonstop flights,** which require no change of plane. If possible, **avoid connecting flights,** which stop at least once and can involve a change of plane, even though the flight number remains the same; if the first leg is late, the second waits.

For better service, **fly smaller or regional carriers,** which often have higher passenger satisfaction ratings. Sometimes they have such inflight amenities as leather seats or greater legroom and they often have better food.

CUTTING COSTS

The Sunday travel section of most newspapers is a good place to look for deals.

MAJOR AIRLINES➢ The least-expensive airfares from the major airlines are priced for round-trip travel and are subject to restrictions. Usually, you must **book in advance and buy the ticket within 24 hours** to get cheaper fares, and you may have to **stay over a Saturday night.** The lowest fare is subject to availability, and only a small percentage of the plane's total seats is sold at that price. It's smart to **call a number of airlines,** and when you are quoted a good price, book it on the spot—the same fare may not be available on the same flight the next day. Airlines generally allow you to change your return date for a $25 to $50 fee. If you don't use your ticket, you can apply the cost toward the purchase of a new ticket, again for a small charge. However, most low-fare tickets are nonrefundable. To get the lowest airfare, **check different routings.** If your destination has more than one gateway, **compare prices to different airports.**

FROM THE U.K.➢ To save money on flights, **look into an APEX or Super-PEX ticket.** APEX tickets must be booked in advance and have certain restrictions. Super-PEX tickets can be purchased right at the airport.

BUS TRAVEL

WMATA's red, white, and blue Metrobuses crisscross the city and nearby suburbs, with some routes running 24 hours a day. All bus rides within the District are $1.10. Free transfers, good for 1½ to 2 hours, are available on buses and in Metro stations. Bus-to-bus transfers are accepted at designated Metrobus transfer points.

Pick up rail-to-bus transfers before boarding the train; there may be a transfer charge when boarding the bus. There are no bus-to-rail transfers.

BUSINESS HOURS

Banks are generally open weekdays 9–3. On Friday many stay open until 5 or close at 2 and open again from 4 to 6. Very few banks have lobby hours on Saturday.

Museums are usually open daily 10–5:30; some have extended hours on Thursday. Many private museums are closed Monday or Tuesday, and some museums in government office buildings are closed weekends. The Smithsonian (☞ Chapter 2) often sets extended spring and summer hours for some of its museums.

Stores are generally open Monday–Saturday 10–7 (or 8). Some have extended hours on Thursday and many—especially those in shopping or tourist areas such as Georgetown—open Sunday anywhere from 10 to noon and close at 5 or 6.

CAR RENTAL

CUTTING COSTS

To get the best deal, **book through a travel agent who is willing to shop around.** When pricing cars, **ask where the rental lot is located.** Some off-airport locations offer lower rates—even though their lots are only minutes away from the terminal via complimentary

shuttle. You also may want to **price local car-rental companies,** whose rates may be lower still, although service and maintenance standards may not be as high as those of a national firm. Ask your agent to **look for fly-drive packages,** which also save you money, and **ask if local taxes are included** in the rental or fly-drive price. These can be as high as 20% in some destinations. Don't forget to find out about required deposits, cancellation penalties, drop-off charges, and the cost of any required insurance coverage.

Also **ask your travel agent about a company's customer-service record.** How has it responded to late plane arrivals and vehicle mishaps? Are there often lines at the rental counter, and—if you're traveling during a holiday period—does a confirmed reservation guarantee you a car?

INSURANCE

When driving a rented car, you are generally responsible for any damage to or loss of the rental vehicle, as well as any property damage or personal injury that you cause. Before you rent, **see what coverage you already have** under the terms of your personal auto insurance policy and credit cards.

For about $14 a day, rental companies sell protection, known as a collision- or loss-damage waiver (CDW or LDW), that eliminates your liability for damage to the car; it's always optional and should never be automatically added to your bill.

In most states, the renter's personal auto insurance or other liability insurance covers damage to third parties. Only when the damage exceeds the renter's own insurance coverage does the car-rental company pay. If you do not have auto insurance or an umbrella insurance policy that covers damage to third parties, purchasing CDW or LDW is highly recommended.

U.K. CITIZENS

In the United States you must be 21 to rent a car; rates may be higher if you're under 25. You'll pay extra for child seats (about $3 per day), compulsory for children under five, and for additional drivers (about $2 per day). To pick up your reserved car you will need the reservation voucher, a passport, a U.K. driver's license, and a travel policy that covers each driver.

SURCHARGES

To avoid a hefty refueling fee, **fill the tank just before you turn in the car**—but be aware that gas stations near the rental outlet may overcharge.

CUSTOMS & DUTIES

To speed your clearance through customs, **keep receipts for all your purchases abroad** and **be ready to show the inspector what you've**
bought. If you feel that you've been incorrectly or unfairly charged a duty, you can **appeal assessments in dispute.** First ask to see a supervisor. If you are still unsatisfied, **write to the port director** your point of entry, sending your customs receipt and any other appropriate documentation. The address will be listed on your receipt. If you still don't get satisfaction, you can take your case to customs headquarters in Washington.

IN WASHINGTON

British visitors age 21 or over may import the following into the United States: 200 cigarettes or 50 cigars or 2 kilograms of tobacco; 1 U.S. liter of alcohol; gifts with a total value of $100. Restricted items include meat products, seeds, plants, and fruits. Never carry illegal drugs.

BACK HOME

IN CANADA➤ If you've been out of Canada for at least seven days, you may bring in C$500 worth of goods duty-free. If you've been away for fewer than seven days but for more than 48 hours, the duty-free allowance drops to C$200; if your trip lasts between 24 and 48 hours, the allowance is C$50. You cannot pool allowances with family members. Goods claimed under the C$500 exemption may follow you by mail; those claimed under the lesser exemptions must accompany you.

Alcohol and tobacco products may be included in the seven-day and 48-hour exemptions but not in the 24-hour exemption. If you meet the age requirements of the province or territory through which you reenter Canada, you may bring in, duty-free, 1.14 liters (40 imperial ounces) of wine or liquor or 24 12-ounce cans or bottles of beer or ale. If you are 16 or older, you may bring in, duty-free, 200 cigarettes, 50 cigars or cigarillos, and 400 tobacco sticks or 400 grams of manufactured tobacco. Alcohol and tobacco must accompany you on your return.

An unlimited number of gifts with a value of up to C$60 each may be mailed to Canada duty-free. These do not affect your duty-free allowance on your return. Label the package "Unsolicited Gift— Value Under $60." Alcohol and tobacco are excluded.

IN THE U.K.➤ From countries outside the EU, including the United States, you may import, duty-free, 200 cigarettes, 100 cigarillos, 50 cigars, or 250 grams of tobacco; 1 liter of spirits or 2 liters of fortified or sparkling wine or liqueurs; 2 liters of still table wine; 60 milliliters of perfume; 250 milliliters of toilet water; plus £136 worth of other goods, including gifts and souvenirs.

DISABILITIES & ACCESSIBILITY

Accessibility continues to improve in D.C. The Metro has excellent facilities for visitors with vision and hearing impairments or mobility problems. Virtually all streets have wide, level sidewalks with curb cuts, though in Georgetown the brick-paved terrain can be bumpy. Most museums and monuments are accessible to visitors using wheelchairs.

DRIVING

Think twice before bringing or renting a car; traffic is horrendous, especially at rush hours, and driving is often confusing, with many lanes and some entire streets changing direction suddenly at certain times of day.

The traffic lights in Washington sometimes stymie visitors. Most of the lights don't hang down over the middle of the streets but stand at the sides of intersections. Radar detectors are illegal in Virginia and the District.

INSURANCE

Travel insurance can protect your monetary investment, replace your luggage and its contents, or provide for medical coverage should you fall ill during your trip. Most tour operators, travel agents, and insurance agents sell specialized health-and-accident, flight, trip-cancellation, and luggage insurance as well as comprehensive policies with some or all of these coverages. Comprehensive policies may also reimburse you for delays due to weather—an important consideration if you're traveling during the winter months. Some health-insurance policies do not cover pre-existing conditions, but waivers may be available in specific cases. Coverage is sold by the companies listed in Important Contacts; these companies act as the policy's administrators. The actual insurance is usually underwritten by a well-known name, such as The Travelers or Continental Insurance.

Before you make any purchase, **review your existing health and homeowner's policies** to find out whether they cover expenses incurred while traveling.

BAGGAGE

Airline liability for baggage is limited to $1,250 per person on domestic flights. On international flights, it amounts to $9.07 per pound or $20 per kilogram for checked baggage (roughly $640 per 70-pound bag) and $400 per passenger for unchecked baggage. Insurance for losses exceeding the terms of your airline ticket can be bought directly from the airline at check-in for about $10 per $1,000 of coverage; note that it excludes a rather extensive list of items, shown on your airline ticket.

COMPREHENSIVE

Comprehensive insurance policies include all the coverages described above plus some that may not be available in more specific policies. If you have purchased an expensive vacation, especially one that involves travel abroad, comprehensive insurance is a must; **look for policies that include trip delay insurance,** which will protect you in the event that weather problems cause you to miss your flight, tour, or cruise. A few insurers will also sell you a waiver for preexisting medical conditions. Some of the companies that offer both these features are Access America, Carefree Travel, Travel Insured International, and TravelGuard (☞ Important Contacts).

FLIGHT

You should **think twice before buying flight insurance.** Often purchased as a last-minute impulse at the airport, it pays a lump sum when a plane crashes, either to a beneficiary if the insured dies or sometimes to a surviving passenger who loses his or her eyesight or a limb. Supplementing the airlines' coverage described in the limits-of-liability paragraphs on your ticket, it's expensive and basically unnecessary. Charging an airline ticket to a major credit card often automatically provides you with coverage that may also extend to travel by bus, train, and ship.

U.K. TRAVELERS

According to the Association of British Insurers, a trade association representing 450 insurance companies, it's wise to **buy extra medical coverage when you visit the United States.** You can buy an annual travel insurance policy valid for most vacations during the year in which it's purchased. If you are pregnant or have a preexisting medical condition, make sure you're covered before buying such a policy.

TRIP

Without insurance, you will lose all or most of your money if you cancel your trip regardless of the reason. Especially if your airline ticket, cruise, or package tour is nonrefundable and cannot be changed, it's essential that you **buy trip-cancellation-and-interruption insurance.** When considering how much coverage you need, look for a policy that will cover the cost of your trip plus the nondiscounted price of a one-way airline ticket should you need to return home early. Read the fine print carefully, especially sections that define "family member" and "preexisting medical conditions." Also **consider default or bankruptcy insurance,** which protects you against a supplier's failure to deliver. Be aware, however, that if you buy such a policy from a travel agency, tour operator, airline, or cruise line, it may not cover default by the firm in question.

MONEY

ATMS

CASH ADVANCES➤ Before leaving home, **make sure that your credit cards have been programmed for ATM use.**

PASSPORTS & VISAS

CANADIANS

No passport is necessary to enter the United States.

U.K. CITIZENS

British citizens need a valid passport to enter the United States. If you are staying for fewer than 90 days and traveling on a vacation, with a return or onward ticket, you probably will not need a visa. However, you will need to fill out the Visa Waiver Form, 1-94W, supplied by the airline.

It is advisable that you **leave one photocopy of your passport's data page** with someone at home and keep another with you, separated from your passport, while traveling. If you lose your passport, promptly call the nearest embassy or consulate and the local police; having the data page information can speed replacement.

SENIOR-CITIZEN DISCOUNTS

To qualify for age-related discounts, **mention your senior-citizen status up front** when booking hotel reservations, not when checking out, and before you're seated in restaurants, not when paying the bill. Note that discounts may be limited to certain menus, days, or hours. When renting a car, **ask about promotional car-rental discounts**—they can net even lower costs than your senior-citizen discount.

SUBWAY TRAVEL

The WMATA provides bus and subway service in the District and in the Maryland and Virginia suburbs. The Metro, opened in 1976, is one of the country's cleanest and safest subway systems. Trains run weekdays 5:30 AM–midnight, weekends 8 AM–midnight. During the weekday rush hours (5:30–9:30 AM and 3–8 PM), trains come along every six minutes. At other times and on weekends and holidays, trains run about every 12–15 minutes. The base fare is $1.10; the actual price you pay depends on the time of day and the distance traveled. Children under age five ride free when accompanied by a paying passenger, but there is a maximum of two children per paying adult.

Buy your ticket at the Farecard machines; they accept coins and crisp $1, $5, $10, or $20 bills. The Farecard should be inserted into the turnstile to enter the platform. **Make sure you hang onto the card—you'll need it to exit at your destination.**

Some Washingtonians report that the Farecard's magnetic strip interferes with the strips on ATM cards and credit cards, so **keep the cards separated in your pocket or wallet.**

DISCOUNT PASSES

For $5 you can **buy a pass that allows unlimited trips for one day.** It's good all day on weekends, on holidays, and after 9:30 AM on weekdays. Passes are available at Metro Sales Outlets (including the Metro Center station) and at many hotels, banks, and Safeway and Giant grocery stores.

TAXIS

Taxis in the District are not metered; they operate instead on a curious zone system. **Before you set off, ask your cab driver how much the fare will be.** The basic single rate for traveling within one zone is $3.20. There is an extra $1.25 charge for each additional passenger and a $1 surcharge during the 4–6:30 PM rush hour. Bulky suitcases are charged at a higher rate, and a $1.50 surcharge is tacked on when you phone for a cab. Maryland and Virginia taxis are metered but are not allowed to take passengers between points in Washington.

Also *see* Airport Transfers *and* Taxis *in* Important Contacts, *above.*

TELEPHONES

LONG-DISTANCE

The long-distance services of AT&T, MCI, and Sprint make calling home relatively convenient and let you avoid hotel surcharges; typically, you dial an 800 number in the United States.

WHEN TO GO

Washington has two delightful seasons: spring and autumn. In spring, the city's ornamental fruit trees are budding, and its many gardens are in bloom. By autumn, most of the summer crowds have left and visitors can enjoy the museums, galleries, and timeless monuments in peace. Summers can be uncomfortably hot and humid. Winter witnesses the lighting of the National Christmas Tree and countless historic-house tours, but the weather is often bitter, with a handful of modest snowstorms that bring the city to a standstill. If you're interested in government, visit when Congress is in session.

CLIMATE

What follows are the average daily maximum and minimum temperatures for Washington.

Jan.	47F	8C	May	76F	24C	Sept.	79F	26C
	34	− 1		58	14		61	16
Feb.	47F	8C	June	85F	29C	Oct.	70F	21C
	31	− 1		65	18		52	11
Mar.	56F	13C	July	88F	31C	Nov.	56F	13C
	38	3		70	21		41	5
Apr.	67F	19C	Aug.	86F	30C	Dec.	47F	8C
	47	8		68	20		32	0

1 Destination: Washington, D.C.

AMERICA'S HOMETOWN

TO A SURPRISING DEGREE, life in Washington is not that different from life elsewhere in the country. People are born here, grow up here, get jobs here—by no means invariably with the federal government—and go on to have children, who repeat the cycle. Very often, they live out their lives without ever testifying before Congress, being indicted for influence peddling, or attending a state dinner at the White House.

Which is not to say that the federal government does not cast a long shadow over the city. Among Washington's 570,000 inhabitants are an awful lot of lawyers, journalists, and people who include the word "policy" in their job titles. It's just that D.C. is much more of a hometown than most tourists realize.

Just a few blocks away from the monuments and museums on the Mall are residential and business districts whose scale is very human. The houses are a crazy quilt of architectural styles, kept in linear formation by rows of lush trees. On the commercial streets, bookstores and ethnic groceries abound.

Redevelopment has left its mark. Fourteenth Street was once the capital's red-light district. The city was determined to clean up the strip, and to everyone's surprise it succeeded. Nor is much left of the tacky commercial district around Ninth and F streets. Washington's original downtown deteriorated when the city's center shifted to the west; the "new" downtown is found on Connecticut Avenue and K Street. But the "old" downtown is being rejuvenated. The department stores that once drew crowds with their window displays have been renovated; there are new hotels and office buildings; and as the construction dust clears, the area is looking pretty good.

Many people who come here are worried about crime. Crime is certainly a major problem, as it is in other big cities, but Washington is not nearly as dangerous as its well-publicized homicide rate might lead you to believe. Most visitors have relatively little to fear. The drug-related shootings that have in the past made Washington a murder capital generally take place in remote sections of the city. Unless you go seeking out the drug markets, there isn't much chance you'll get caught in the cross fire of rival drug gangs.

Crimes against property are more widespread, but still far from ubiquitous. Unlike New York, Washington is not full of expert pickpockets; nor is it plagued by gold-chain snatchers.

The city's Metro is generally safe, even at night. However, if you have to walk from a stop in a neighborhood that isn't well lit and trafficked, you probably should invest in a taxi. Of course, even exercising normal prudence, it is still possible that you will have an encounter with someone who believes that what's yours ought to be his. If that happens, don't argue.

Your attachment to the contents of your wallet is certain to be tested in another way, however. Panhandlers are now a fixture of the cityscape, and there is no avoiding their importunities. How you respond to them is a matter only your conscience can advise you on. Wealth and poverty have always coexisted in America's hometown; but poverty is now omnipresent, wearing a very human face.

— By Deborah Papier

A native of Washington, Deborah Papier has worked as an editor and writer for numerous local newspapers and magazines.

HISTORY AT A GLANCE

1608 Captain John Smith sails from Jamestown up the Potomac River. Colonization follows.

1775–83 American Revolutionary War.

1788 U.S. Constitution ratified.

1789 New York is the capital; George Washington becomes the first U.S. president.

1790 Philadelphia is now the capital; but in return for the South's assumption of the North's Revolutionary War debt, George Washington will select a Southern capital site.

1792 White House construction begins.

1793 Capitol Building construction begins.

1800 Congress relocates from Philadelphia; John Adams, elected in **1797,** moves into an unfinished White House.

1803 The city's population is 3,000.

1812–15 War of 1812. In **1814,** British burn Washington, including such landmarks as the White House and the Capitol; storms save the city from total destruction.

1846 Smithsonian Institution established.

1861–65 Civil War. Lincoln assassinated in **1865.**

1900 The city's population is 300,000.

1912 Cherry trees, gifts from Japan, are planted.

1914–18 World War I (United States enters in **1917**).

1929–39 Great Depression.

1939–45 World War II (United States enters in **1941**).

1943 Pentagon completed.

1963 President Kennedy assassinated in Dallas.

1972 Watergate break-in.

1976 Metrorail service begins.

1994 The city's population is 570,000.

PRESIDENTS

George Washington	(1789–97)
John Adams	(1797–1801)
Thomas Jefferson	(1801–09)
James Madison	(1809–17)
James Monroe	(1817–25)
John Quincy Adams	(1825–29)
Andrew Jackson	(1829–37)
Martin Van Buren	(1837–41)
William Henry Harrison	(1841)
John Tyler	(1841–45)
James Knox Polk	(1845–49)
Zachary Taylor	(1849–50)
Millard Fillmore	(1850–53)
Franklin Pierce	(1853–57)
James Buchanan	(1857–61)
Abraham Lincoln	(1861–65)
Andrew Johnson	(1865–69)
Ulysses Simpson Grant	(1869–77)
Rutherford Birchard Hayes	(1877–81)
James Abram Garfield	(1881)
Chester Alan Arthur	(1881–85)
(Stephen) Grover Cleveland	(1885–89)
Benjamin Harrison	(1889–93)
(Stephen) Grover Cleveland	(1893–97)
William McKinley	(1897–1901)
Theodore Roosevelt	(1901–1909)

William Howard Taft	(1909–13)
(Thomas) Woodrow Wilson	(1913–21)
Warren Gamaliel Harding	(1921–23)
(John) Calvin Coolidge	(1923–29)
Herbert Clark Hoover	(1929–33)
Franklin Delano Roosevelt	(1933–45)
Harry S. Truman	(1945–53)
Dwight David Eisenhower	(1953–61)
John Fitzgerald Kennedy	(1961–63)
Lyndon Baines Johnson	(1963–69)
Richard Milhous Nixon	(1969–74)
Gerald Rudolph Ford	(1974–77)
James Earl (Jimmy) Carter	(1977–81)
Ronald Wilson Reagan	(1981–89)
George Herbert Walker Bush	(1989–93)
William Jefferson (Bill) Clinton	(1993–)

2 Exploring Washington

By John F.
Kelly

Updated
by Bruce
Walker

TIRED OF ITS NOMADIC EXISTENCE after having set up shop in eight different locations, Congress voted in 1785 to establish a permanent "Federal town." Northern lawmakers wanted the capital on the Delaware River while southerners wanted it on the Potomac. A deal was struck when Virginia's Thomas Jefferson agreed to support the proposal that the federal government assume the war debts of the colonies if New York's Alexander Hamilton and other northern legislators would agree to locate the capital on the banks of the Potomac. George Washington himself selected the exact site of the capital, a diamond-shape, 100-square-mile plot that encompassed the confluence of the Potomac and Anacostia rivers, not far from the president's estate at Mount Vernon. To give the young city a bit of a head start, Washington included the already thriving tobacco ports of Alexandria, Virginia, and Georgetown, Maryland, in the District of Columbia.

Pierre-Charles L'Enfant, a young French engineer who had fought in the Revolution, offered his services in creating a capital "magnificent enough to grace a great nation." He wrote that his plan would "leave room for that aggrandizement and embellishment which the increase in the wealth of the nation will permit it to pursue at any period, however remote." At times it must have seemed remote indeed, for the town grew so slowly that when Charles Dickens visited Washington in 1842 what he saw were "spacious avenues that begin in nothing and lead nowhere; streets a mile long that only want houses, roads, and inhabitants; public buildings that need but a public to be complete and ornaments of great thoroughfares which need only great thoroughfares to ornament."

It took the Civil War—and every war thereafter—to energize the city, by attracting thousands of new residents and spurring building booms that extended the capital in all directions. Despite the growth and despite the fact that blacks have always played an important role in the city's history (black mathematician Benjamin Banneker surveyed the land with Pierre L'Enfant in the 18th century), Washington today remains essentially segregated. Whites—who account for about 30% of the population—reside mostly in northwest Washington. Blacks live largely east of Rock Creek Park and south of the Anacostia River.

It's a city of other unfortunate contrasts: Citizens of the capital of the free world couldn't vote in a presidential election until 1964, weren't granted limited home rule until 1974, and are represented in Congress by a single nonvoting delegate (though in 1990 residents elected two "shadow" senators, one of whom is political gadfly Jesse Jackson). Homeless people sleep on steam grates next to multimillion-dollar government buildings, and a flourishing drug trade has earned Washington the dubious distinction of murder capital of the United States. Though it's little consolation to those affected, most crime is restricted to neighborhoods far from the areas visited by tourists.

Still, there's no denying that Washington, the world's first planned capital city, is also one of its most beautiful. And though the federal government dominates the city psychologically as much as the Washington Monument dominates it physically, there are parts of the capital where you can leave politics behind. The walks that follow will take you through the monumental city, the governmental city, and the residential city. As you walk, look for evidence of L'Enfant's hand, still present despite growing pains and frequent deviations from his plan. His Washington was to be a city of vistas—pleasant views that would shift and change from block to block, a marriage of geometry and art. It remains this way today. Like its main industry, politics, Washington's design is a constantly changing kaleidoscope that invites contemplation from all angles.

The Mall

The Mall is the heart of nearly every visitor's trip to Washington. With nearly a dozen diverse museums ringing the expanse of green, it's the closest thing the capital has to a theme park (unless you count the federal government itself, which has uncharitably been called "Disneyland on the Potomac"). As at a theme park, you may have to stand in an occasional line, but unlike the amusements at Disney-

Exploring Washington, D.C. *(Boxes Refer to Detail Maps)*

Georgetown

Dupont Circle and Foggy Bottom

The White House Area

California St.

S St.

Decatur Pl.

R St.

Sheridan Circle

R St.

Q St.

Massachusetts Ave.

P St.

O St.

30th St.
29th St.
28th St.
27th St.

Rock Creek

M St.

L St.

Washington Circle

Pennsylvania Ave.

25th St.

24th St.
23rd St.
22nd St.

Virginia Ave.

Florida Ave.

22nd St.
21st St.
20th St.
19th St.

New Hampshire Ave.

Connecticut Ave.

M Dupont Circle

Church St.

P St.

O St.

N St.

L St.

K St.

G St.

F St.

E St.

18th St.
17th St.
16th St.

S St.

Corcoran St.

Church St.

Scott Circle

Thomas Circle

15th St.
14th St.

Rhode Island Ave.

New Hampshire Ave.

29

29

50

M

M

H St.

New York Ave.

The White House

D St.

C St.

15th St.
14th St.

Constitution Ave.

Lincoln Memorial

Reflecting Pool

Arlington Memorial Br.

Independence Ave.

Kutz Br.

Washington Monument

Columbia Island

West Potomac Park

Ohio Dr.

W. Basin Dr.

Tidal Basin

Outlet Br.

Lady Bird Johnson Park

Potomac River

Jefferson Memorial

1

395

To Alexandria

The Monuments

NW ◆ NE

S St.

Vermont Ave.

S St.

Florida Ave.

Rhode Island Ave.

R St.

Q St.

New Jersey Ave.

Lincoln Rd.

R St.

Q St.

P St.

9th St.

3rd St.

O St.

O St.

8th St.

6th St.

5th St.

4th St.

1st St.

N St.

New York Ave.

N St.

10th St.

12th St.

M St.

North Capitol St.

M St.

3rd St.

L St.

sachusetts Ave.

7th St.

Mt. Vernon Square

Massachusetts Ave.

I St.

H St.

Old Downtown and Federal Triangle

Capitol Hill

G St.

2nd St.

Union Station

F St.

Columbus Memorial Fountain

E St.

395

D St.

Stanton Park

Pennsylvania Ave.

Louisiana Ave.

Constitution Ave.

National Gallery of Art

NE

E. Capitol St.

Madison Dr.

Smithsonian Institution

THE MALL

Jefferson Dr.

National Air and Space Museum

US Capitol

SE

Independence Ave.

Maryland Ave.

Folger Park

C St.

Canal St.

The Mall

D St.

E St.

Southwest Fwy.

395

G St.

G St.

0   550 yards

0   500 meters

Virginia Ave.

New Jersey Ave.

I St.

ancis Case emorial Br.

Washington Canal

N

SW ◆ SE

land almost everything you'll see here is free. (You may, however, need free, timed-entry tickets to some of the more popular traveling exhibitions. These are usually available at the museum information desk or by phone, for a service charge, from TicketMaster, at 202/432–7328.)

Of course, the Mall is more than just a front yard for all these museums. Bounded on the north and south by Constitution and Independence avenues, and on the east and west by 3rd and 14th streets, it's a picnicking park and a jogging path, an outdoor stage for festivals and fireworks, and America's town green. Nine of the Smithsonian Institution's fourteen museums in the Capitol lie within these boundaries. (The nearest Metro stops are Smithsonian, Archives/Navy Memorial, and L'Enfant Plaza).

Numbers in the text correspond to numbers in the margin and on the Mall map.

Sights to See

⑫ **Arthur M. Sackler Gallery.** When Charles Freer endowed the gallery that bears his name (☞ *below*), he insisted on a few conditions: Objects in the collection could not be loaned out, nor could objects from outside the collections be put on display. Because of the latter restriction it was necessary to build a second, complementary museum to house the Oriental art collection of Arthur M. Sackler, a wealthy medical researcher and publisher who began collecting Asian art as a student in the 1940s. Sackler allowed Smithsonian curators to select 1,000 items from his ample collection and pledged $4 million toward the construction of the museum. The collection includes works from China, the Indian subcontinent, Persia, Thailand, and Indonesia. Articles in the permanent collection include Chinese ritual bronzes, jade ornaments from the 3rd millennium BC, Persian manuscripts, and Indian paintings in gold, silver, lapis lazuli, and malachite. ✉ *1050 Independence Ave. SW,* ☎ *202/357–2700, TTY 202/357–1729.* 🎫 *Free.* ☉ *Daily 10–5:30. Metro: Smithsonian.*

❷ **Arts and Industries Building.** Exhibiting a rich collection of American Victoriana, this was the second Smithsonian museum to be constructed. In 1876 Philadelphia hosted the United States International Exposition in honor of the nation's Centennial. After the festivities, scores of exhibitors donated their displays to the federal government. In order to house the objects that had suddenly come its way, the Smithsonian commissioned this redbrick and sandstone building. Designed by Adolph Cluss, the building was originally called the United States National Museum, the name that is still engraved in stone above the doorway. It was finished in 1881, just in time to host President James Garfield's inaugural ball. Many of the objects on display—which include carriages, tools, furnishings, printing presses, even a steam locomotive—are from the original Philadelphia Centennial. ⊠ *900 Jefferson Dr. SW,* ☎ *202/357-2700, TTY 202/357-1729.* 🖅 *Free.* ☉ *Daily 10-5:30. Metro: Smithsonian.*

🖐 **❾** **Bureau of Engraving and Printing.** Paper money has been printed in this huge building since 1914, when they stopped printing it in the Auditor's Building. Despite the fact that there are no free samples, the 30-minute guided tour of the bureau—which takes visitors past presses that turn out some $450 million a day—is one of the city's most popular. In addition to all the paper currency in the United States, stamps, military certificates, and presidential invitations are printed here too. ⊠ *14th and C Sts. SW,* ☎ *202/874-3019.* 🖅 *Free; Apr. 3-Sept., same-day timed-entry passes issued starting at 7:45* AM *at Raoul Wallenberg Pl. SW entrance.* ☉ *Weekdays 9-2. Metro: Smithsonian.*

❿ **Department of Agriculture.** While there's nothing of interest to tourists inside, this sprawling complex is too gargantuan to ignore. The home of a major governmental agency responsible for setting and carrying out the nation's agricultural policies, it comprises two buildings. The older building, on the north side of Independence Avenue, was started in 1905. The cornices on the north side of this white-marble building feature some of the plants the department keeps an eye on. The newer building south of Independence Avenue covers two city blocks (an example, perhaps, of big government). ⊠ *Independence Ave. between 12th and 14th Sts. SW. Metro: Smithsonian.*

⓫ **Freer Gallery of Art.** One of the world's finest collections of masterpieces from Asia, the Smithsonian's Freer Gallery of Art was made possible by an endowment from Detroit

14

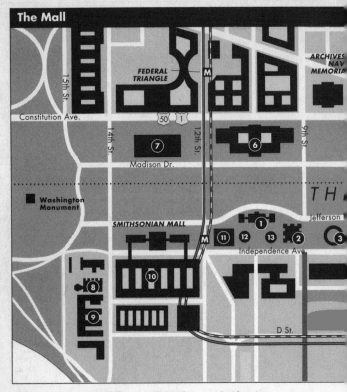

The Mall

FEDERAL TRIANGLE

ARCHIVES NAV MEMORIA

Constitution Ave.

15th St.

14th St.

12th St.

9th St.

Madison Dr.

⑦

⑥

Washington Monument

TH

SMITHSONIAN MALL

Jefferson

⑪ ⑫ ⑬ ① ② ③

Independence Ave.

⑩

⑧

⑨

D St.

Arthur M. Sackler Gallery, **12**

Arts and Industries Building, **2**

Bureau of Engraving and Printing, **9**

Department of Agriculture, **10**

Freer Gallery of Art, **11**

Hirshhorn Museum and Sculpture Garden, **3**

National Air and Space Museum, **4**

National Gallery of Art, **5**

National Museum of African Art, **13**

National Museum of American History, **7**

National Museum of Natural History, **6**

Smithsonian Institution Building, **1**

United States Holocaust Memorial Museum, **8**

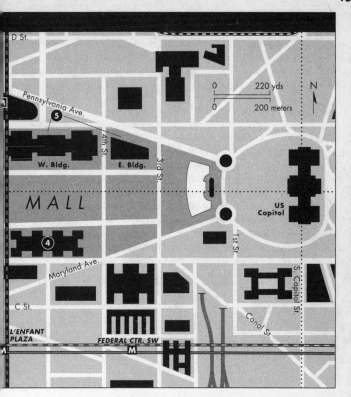

D St.

Pennsylvania Ave.

⑤

4th St.

W. Bldg.

E. Bldg.

3rd St.

0   220 yds
0   200 meters

N

MALL

④

US
Capitol

1st St.

Maryland Ave.

C St.

S. Capitol St.

L'ENFANT
PLAZA

FEDERAL CTR. SW

Canal St.

M   M

industrialist Charles L. Freer, who retired in 1900 and devoted the rest of his life to collecting art. Opened in 1923, four years after its benefactor's death, its collection includes more than 26,000 works of art from the Far and Near East, including Asian porcelains, Japanese screens, Chinese paintings and bronzes, Korean stoneware, and examples of Islamic art.

Freer's friend James McNeill Whistler introduced him to Asian art, and the American painter is represented in the vast collection. On display in Gallery 12 is the "Peacock Room," a blue-and-gold dining room decorated with painted leather, wood, and canvas and designed by Whistler for a British shipping magnate. Freer paid $30,000 for the entire room and moved it from London to the United States in 1904. The works of other American artists Freer felt were influenced by the Orient also are on display. ⊠ *12th St. and Jefferson Dr. SW,* ☏ *202/357–2700, TTY 202/357–1729.* 🖼 *Free.* ☉ *Daily 10–5:30. Metro: Smithsonian.*

❸ Hirshhorn Museum and Sculpture Garden. An architecturally striking but aesthetically controversial building that opened in 1974, the Hirschhorn manages a collection that includes 4,000 paintings and drawings and 2,000 sculptures donated by Joseph H. Hirshhorn, a Latvian-born immigrant who made his fortune in this country running uranium mines. American artists such as Eakins, Pollock, Rothko, and Stella are represented, as are modern European and Latin masters, including Francis Bacon, Fernando Botero, Magritte, Miró, and Victor Vasarely.

The Hirshhorn's impressive sculpture collection is arranged in the open spaces between the museum's concrete piers and across Jefferson Drive in the sunken **Sculpture Garden.** The display in the Sculpture Garden includes one of the largest public American collections of works by Henry Moore (58 sculptures), as well as works by Honoré Daumier, Max Ernst, Alberto Giacometti, Pablo Picasso, and Man Ray. Auguste Rodin's *Burghers of Calais* is a highlight. ⊠ *Independence Ave. and 7th St. SW,* ☏ *202/357–2700, TTY 202/357–1729.* 🖼 *Free.* ☉ *Daily 10–5:30, sculpture garden open daily 7:30–dusk. Metro: Smithsonian.*

★ ☕ ❹ **National Air and Space Museum.** Opened in 1976, Air and Space is the most visited museum in the world, attracting some 12 million people each year. (It's thought to be the most-visited building on earth.) Twenty-three galleries tell the story of aviation from the earliest human attempts at flight. Suspended from the ceiling like plastic models in a child's room are dozens of aircraft, including the actual "Wright Flyer" that Wilbur Wright piloted over the sands of Kitty Hawk, North Carolina; Charles Lindbergh's "Spirit of St. Louis"; the X-1 rocket plane in which Chuck Yeager broke the sound barrier; and the X-15, the fastest plane ever built.

Other highlights include a backup model of the Skylab orbital workshop that visitors can walk through; the Voyager airplane that Dick Rutan and Jeana Yeager flew nonstop around the world; the Lockheed Vega piloted by Amelia Earhart in 1932 in the first solo transatlantic flight by a woman; and the U.S.S. *Enterprise* model used in the "Star Trek" TV show, which is currently unviewable due to repairs. Visitors can also touch a piece of the moon: a 4-billion-year-old slice of rock collected by Apollo 17 astronauts. ✉ *Jefferson Dr. and 6th St. SW,* ☎ *202/357–2700, TTY 202/357–1729.* 🎟 *Free.* ☉ *Daily 10–5:30, extended summer hrs determined annually. Metro: Smithsonian.*

NEED A BREAK? Two restaurants are at the eastern end of the National Air and Space Museum: **The Wright Place** is a table-service restaurant that takes reservations (☎ 202/371–8777); the **Flight Line** is a self-service cafeteria. They each have a large selection of foods, but at peak times lines can be long.

★ ❺ **National Gallery of Art.** The two buildings of the National Gallery hold one of the world's foremost collections of paintings, sculptures, and graphics. If you want to view the museum's holdings in (more or less) chronological order, it's best to start your exploration of this magnificent gallery in the **West Building**. Opened in 1941, the domed building was a gift to the nation from financier Andrew Mellon. He had long collected great works of art, acquiring some on his frequent trips to Europe. In 1931, when the Soviet government was short on cash and selling off many of its art treasures, Mellon stepped in and bought more than $6 million worth of old masters, including *The Alba Madonna* by Raphael and Botticelli's *Adoration of the Magi*. Mellon promised his collection to America in 1936, the year before his death. He also donated the funds for the construction of the huge gallery and resisted suggestions it be named after him.

The East Building opened in 1978 in response to the changing needs of the National Gallery. The atrium of the East Building is dominated by two massive works of art: Alexander Calder's mobile *Untitled* and *Woman*, a huge wall-hanging by Joan Miró. The galleries here generally display modern art, though the East Building serves as a home for major temporary exhibitions that span years and artistic styles. ⊠ *Constitution Ave. between 3rd and 7th Sts. NW,* ☎ *202/737–4215, TTY 202/842–6176.* ☜ *Free.* ☉ *Mon.–Sat. 10–5, Sun. 11–6. Metro: Archives/Navy Memorial.*

NEED A BREAK?   Two restaurants on the concourse level between the East and West buildings of the National Gallery offer bleary-eyed and foot-sore museum goers the chance to recharge. The **Buffet** serves a wide variety of soups, sandwiches, salads, hot entrées, and desserts. The **Cascade Café** has a smaller selection, but customers enjoy the soothing effect of the gentle waterfall that splashes against the glass-covered wall. If you're in the East Building, try the Terrace Café; in the West Building, dine in the Garden Café.

---

 ⑬ National Museum of African Art. Founded in 1964 as a private educational institution dedicated to the collection, exhibition, and study of the traditional arts of Africa, this museum now holds a permanent collection of more than 7,000 objects representing hundreds of African cultures. On display are masks, carvings, textiles, and jewelry, all made from materials such as wood, fiber, bronze, ivory, and fired clay. A new permanent exhibit explores the personal objects—chairs, pipes, cups, snuff containers—that were a part of daily life in 19th- and early 20th-century Africa. ⊠ *950 Independence Ave. SW,* ☎ *202/357–4600, TTY 202/357–4814.* ☜ *Free.* ☉ *Daily 10–5:30. Metro: Smithsonian.*

🐾 ❼ **National Museum of American History.** The exhibits here explore America's cultural, political, technical, and scientific past. The incredible diversity of artifacts helps the Smithsonian live up to its nickname as "the Nation's attic." This is the museum that displayed Muhammad Ali's boxing gloves, the Fonz's leather jacket, and the Bunkers' living room furniture from "All in the Family." The exhibits on the first floor emphasize the history of science and technology and include such items as farm machines, antique automobiles, early phonographs, and a 280-ton steam locomotive. The permanent "Science in American Life" exhibit—opened in 1994 and covering a whopping 12,000 square feet—shows how science has shaped American life through such breakthroughs as the mass production of penicillin, the development of plastics, and the birth of the environmental movement. The second floor is devoted to U.S. social and political history and features an exhibit on everyday American life just after the Revolution. A permanent exhibit, "First Ladies: Political Role and Public Image," displays the gowns worn by various presidential wives, but it goes beyond fashion to explore the women behind the satin, lace, and brocade.

Those who want a more interactive visit should stop at two places: In the **Hands On History Room** visitors can ride a high-wheeler bike, harness a mule, or sort mail as it was done on the railroads in the 1870s. In the **Hands On Science Room** you can do one of 25 experiments, including testing a water sample and exploring DNA fingerprinting. ⊠ *Constitution Ave. and 14th St. NW,* ☎ *202/357–2700, TTY 202/357–1729.* 🎟 *Free.* ☉ *Daily 10–5:30, Hands On History room Tues.–Sun. noon–3, Hands On Science room daily 10–5:30, extended spring and summer hrs determined annually. Metro: Smithsonian.*

★ 🐾 ❻ **National Museum of Natural History.** Most of the Smithsonian's collection of objects—some 120 million specimens—are stored in the National Museum of Natural History. It was constructed in 1910, and two wings were added in the '60s. The result is one of the great natural history museums of the world, filled with bones, fossils, stuffed animals, and other natural delights. Exhibits also explore the many ingenious ways that humans adapt to their environment.

The first-floor rotunda is dominated by a stuffed, 8-ton, 13-foot African bull elephant, one of the largest specimens ever found. (The tusks are fiberglass; the original ivory ones were apparently far too heavy for the stuffed elephant to support.) Off to the right is the popular **Dinosaur Hall.** Fossilized skeletons on display range from a 90-foot-long diplodocus to a tiny thesalosaurus neglectus (a small dinosaur so named because its disconnected bones sat forgotten for years in a college drawer before being reassembled).

In the west wing are displays on birds, mammals, and sea life. Many of the preserved specimens are from the collection of animals bagged by Teddy Roosevelt on his trips to Africa. Not everything in the museum is dead, though. The sea-life display features a living coral reef, complete with fish, plants, and simulated waves.

The highlight of the second floor is the **mineral and gem collection.** Objects include the largest sapphire on public display in the country (the Logan Sapphire, 423 carats), the largest uncut diamond (the Oppenheimer Diamond, 253.7 carats), and, of course, the Hope Diamond, a blue gem found in India and reputed to carry a curse (though Smithsonian guides are quick to pooh-pooh this notion). The amazing gem collection is second in value only to the crown jewels of Great Britain. (The Hall of Gems was closed for renovations at press time and is expected to reopen in fall 1997; however, its more spectacular objects will remain on display.)

If you've always wished you could get your hands on the objects behind the glass, stop by the **Discovery Room,** in the northwest corner of the first floor. Here elephant tusks, petrified wood, seashells, rocks, feathers, and other items from the natural world can be handled by children and their parents. ⊠ *Constitution Ave. and 10th Sts. NW,* ☎ *202/357–2700, TTY 202/357–1729.* ⊠ *Free.* ☉ *Daily 10–5:30; Discovery Room Tues.–Fri. noon–2:30, weekends 10:30–3:30; in spring and summer free passes distributed starting at 11:45 weekdays, 10:15 weekends; Naturalist Center Mon.–Sat. 10:30–4; extended spring and summer hrs determined annually. Metro: Smithsonian.*

National Sculpture Garden Ice Rink. In winter, you can rent skates at this circular ice-skating rink, which is located across the Mall directly opposite the National Gallery of Art. Ice cream and other refreshments are available at the green building during the summer. ✉ *7th St. and Constitution Ave. NW,* ☎ *202/371–5340. Metro: Archives/Navy Memorial.*

❶ Smithsonian Institution Building. The first Smithsonian museum constructed, it is better known as the Castle. Although British scientist and founder James Smithson had never visited America, his will stipulated that, should his nephew, Henry James Hungerford, die without an heir, Smithson's entire fortune would go to the United States, "to found at Washington, under the name of the Smithsonian Institution, an establishment for the increase and diffusion of knowledge among men."

Smithson died in 1829, Hungerford in 1835, and in 1838 the United States received $515,169 worth of gold sovereigns. After eight years of congressional debate over the propriety of accepting funds from a private citizen, the Smithsonian Institution was finally established in 1846. The red sandstone, Norman-style headquarters building on Jefferson Drive was completed in 1855 and originally housed all of the Smithsonian's operations, including the science and art collections, research laboratories, and living quarters for the institution's secretary and his family. The building was designed by James Renwick, the architect of St. Patrick's Cathedral in New York City. The statue in front of the Castle's entrance is not of Smithson but of Joseph Henry, the scientist who served as the institution's first secretary. Smithson's body was brought to America in 1904 and is entombed in a small room to the left of the Castle's Mall entrance.

Today the Castle houses Smithsonian administrative offices and is home to the Woodrow Wilson International School for Scholars. To get your bearings or help in deciding which Mall attractions you want to visit, drop by the **Smithsonian Information Center** in the Castle. The Information Center opens at 9 AM, an hour before the other museums open, so you can plan your day on the Mall without wasting valuable sightseeing time. ✉ *1000 Jefferson Dr. SW,* ☎ *202/357–2700, TTY 202/357–1729.* ✆ *Free.* ☉ *Daily 9–5:30; closed Dec. 25. Metro: Smithsonian.*

★ **8**   **United States Holocaust Memorial Museum.** The story of the 11 million Jews, Gypsies, Jehovah's Witnesses, homosexuals, political prisoners, and others killed by the Nazis between 1933 and 1945 is told at this James Ingo Freed-designed museum. The Holocaust is recounted in an almost cinematic fashion, with documentary films, videotaped oral histories, and a collection that includes such items as a German freight car, used to transport Jews from Warsaw to the Treblinka death camp, and the Star of David patches that Jewish prisoners were made to wear. Like the history it covers, the museum can be profoundly disturbing; it is not recommended for visitors under 11. Plan to spend at least four hours here. After this powerful—even wrenching—experience, the adjacent **Hall of Remembrance** provides a space for quiet reflection. ⊠ *100 Raoul Wallenberg Pl. SW (enter from Raoul Wallenberg Pl. or 14th St. SW),* ☎ *202/488–0400; tickets also available through Ticketmaster,* ☎ *202/432–7328.* ⊡ *Free, although same-day timed-entry passes necessary (often not available after 11 AM).* ☉ *Daily 10–5:30. Metro: Smithsonian.*

The Monuments

Washington is a city of monuments. In the middle of traffic circles, on tiny slivers of park, and at street corners and intersections, statues, plaques, and simple blocks of marble honor the generals, politicians, poets, and statesmen who helped shape the nation. The monuments dedicated to the most famous Americans are west of the Mall on ground reclaimed from the marshy flats of the Potomac. This is also the location of Washington's cherry trees, gifts from Japan and focus of a festival each spring.

Numbers in the text correspond to numbers in the margin and on the Monuments map.

Sights to See

Constitution Gardens. Many ideas were proposed to develop a 50-acre site that was once home to "temporary" buildings erected by the Navy before World War I and not removed until after World War II. President Nixon is said to have favored something resembling Copenhagen's Tivoli Gardens. The final design was a little plainer, with paths winding through groves of trees and, on the lake, a tiny island paying tribute to the signers of the Declaration of Independence, their signatures carved into a low stone wall. ⊠ *Constitution Ave. between 17th and 23rd Sts. NW. Metro: Foggy Bottom.*

NEED A BREAK? At the circular **snack bar** just west of the Constitution Gardens lake you can get hot dogs, potato chips, candy bars, soft drinks, and beer at prices lower than those charged by most street vendors.

② Jefferson Memorial. The monument honoring the third president of the United States is the southernmost of the major monuments in the District. Congress decided that Jefferson deserved a monument positioned as prominently as those in honor of Washington and Lincoln, and this spot directly south of the White House seemed ideal. Jefferson had always admired the Pantheon in Rome—the rotundas he designed for the University of Virginia and his own Monticello were inspired by its dome—so architect John Russell Pope drew from the same source when he designed this memorial to our third president. Dedicated in 1943, it houses a statue of Jefferson. Its walls are lined with inscriptions based on his writings. One of the best views of the White House can be seen from the memorial's top steps. ⊠ *Tidal Basin, south bank,* ☎ *202/426–6821.* ☒ *Free.* ◷ *Daily 8 AM–midnight. Metro: Archives/Navy Memorial.*

★ ☙ **③ Lincoln Memorial.** Many people consider the Lincoln Memorial to be the most inspiring monument in the city. This was not always the case. Detractors of the Lincoln Memorial thought it inappropriate that the humble Lincoln be honored with what amounts to a modified but nonetheless rather grandiose Greek temple. The white Colorado-marble memorial was designed by Henry Bacon and completed in 1922. The 36 Doric columns represent the 36 states in the Union at the time of Lincoln's death; the names of the states appear on the frieze above the columns. Above the frieze are the names of the 48 states that comprised the Union when the memorial was dedicated. (Alaska and Hawaii are noted by an inscription on the terrace leading up to the memorial.)

Daniel Chester French's somber statue of the seated president, in the center of the memorial, gazes out over the Reflecting Pool. Though the 19-foot-high sculpture looks as if it were cut from one huge block of stone, it actually comprises 28 interlocking pieces of Georgia marble. Inscribed on the south wall is the Gettysburg Address, and on the north wall is Lincoln's second inaugural address. Above each inscription is a mural painted by Jules Guerin: On the south wall is an angel of truth freeing a slave; the unity of North and South are depicted opposite. The memorial served as a fitting backdrop for Martin Luther King's "I have a dream" speech in 1963.

Many visitors focus only on the Lincoln Memorial, but there is much more to explore in the surrounding area. The **Korean War Veterans Memorial**, between Independence Avenue and the Lincoln Memorial, in a grove of trees called Ash Woods, was dedicated on July 27, 1995—the 42nd anniversary of the Korean War armistice. **The Korean War Veterans Memorial** consists of a column of soldiers marching toward an American flag, along with a reflecting pool and a granite wall etched with war scenes.

Although visiting the area around the Lincoln Memorial during the day allows you to take in an impressive view of the Mall to the east, the best time to see the memorial itself is at night. Spotlights illuminate the outside while inside, light and shadows play across Lincoln's gentle face. ⊠ *West end of Mall,* ☎ *202/426–6895.* ▣ *Free.* ⊙ *24 hrs; staffed daily 8 AM–midnight. Metro: Foggy Bottom.*

❺ **Lockkeeper's House.** The stone Lockkeeper's House is the only remaining monument to Washington's unsuccessful experiment with a canal. L'Enfant's design called for a canal to be dug from the Tiber—a branch of the Potomac that extended from where the Lincoln Memorial is now—across the city to the Capitol and then south to the Anacostia River. (L'Enfant even envisioned the president riding in a ceremonial barge from the White House to the Capitol.) The City Canal became more nuisance than convenience, and by the Civil War it was a foul-smelling cesspool that often overran its banks. The stone building at this corner was the home of the canal's lockkeeper until the 1870s, when the water-

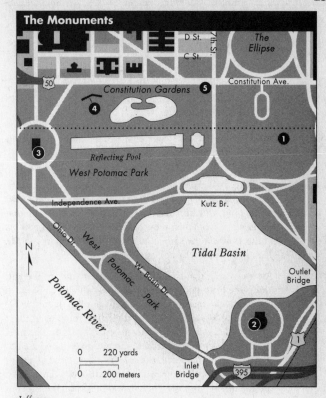

Jefferson
Memorial, **2**

Lincoln
Memorial, **3**

Lockkeeper's
House, **5**

Vietnam
Veterans
Memorial, **4**

Washington
Monument, **1**

way was covered over with B Street, which was renamed
Constitution Avenue in 1932. ⊠ *Constitution Ave. and 17th
St. Metro: Federal Triangle, 5 blocks east on 12th St.*

☾ **Tidal Basin.** This placid pond was part of the Potomac
until 1882, when portions of the river were filled in to improve navigation and create additional parkland, including that upon which the Jefferson Memorial was later built.
Paddleboats have been a fixture on the Tidal Basin for
years. You can rent one at the boathouse on the east side
of the basin, southwest of the Bureau of Engraving.

Walking along the sidewalk that hugs the Tidal Basin,
you'll see two grotesque sculpted heads on the sides of the
Inlet Bridge. The inside walls of the bridge covet two other
interesting sculptures: bronze, human-headed fish that
spout water from their mouths. The bridge was refurbished
in the 1980s at the same time the chief of the park—a Mr.
Jack Fish—was retiring.

After crossing the bridge, you can either walk to the left,
along the Potomac, or continue along the Tidal Basin to
the right. The latter route is somewhat more scenic, especially in April, when the cherry trees are in bloom. The first
batch of these trees arrived from Japan in 1909. The trees
were infected with insects and fungus, however, and the Department of Agriculture ordered them destroyed. A diplomatic crisis was averted when the United States politely asked
the Japanese for another batch, and in 1912 Mrs. William
Howard Taft planted the first tree. The second was planted
by the wife of the Japanese ambassador. About 200 of the
original trees still grow near the Tidal Basin. The trees are
now the centerpiece of Washington's Cherry Blossom Festival, held each spring; they are usually in bloom for about
10–12 days at the beginning of April. ⊠ *Northeast bank
of Tidal Basin,* ☎ *202/484–0206.* ▣ *Paddleboat rental $8
per hr, $1.75 each additional 15 mins.* ☉ *Mid-Apr.–late Nov.,
daily 10–6, weather permitting. Metro: Archives/Navy
Memorial.*

❹ **Vietnam Veterans Memorial.** Renowned for its power to
evoke deep and poignant reflection, the Vietnam Veterans
Memorial was conceived by Jan Scruggs, a former infantry
corporal who served in Vietnam. The stark design by Maya

Ying Lin, a 21-year-old Yale architecture student, was selected in a 1981 competition and brought to fruition in 1982. The names of more than 58,000 Americans are etched on the face of the memorial in the order of their deaths; directories at the entrance and exit to the wall list the names in alphabetical order. ⊠ *Constitution Gardens, 23rd St. and Constitution Ave. NW,* ☎ *202/634–1568.* ⊡ *Free.* ☉ *24 hrs; staffed daily 8 AM–midnight. Metro: Foggy Bottom.*

Vietnam Women's Memorial. After years of debate over its design and necessity, the Vietnam Women's Memorial, honoring the women who served in that conflict, was finally dedicated on Veterans Day 1993. It's a stirring sculpture group consisting of two uniformed women caring for a wounded male soldier while a third woman kneels nearby. ⊠ *Constitution Gardens, southeast of Vietnam Veterans Memorial. Metro: Foggy Bottom.*

❶ Washington Monument. Congress first authorized a monument to General Washington in 1783. In his 1791 plan for the city, Pierre L'Enfant selected a site (the point where a line drawn west from the Capitol crossed one drawn south from the White House), but it wasn't until 1833, after years of quibbling in Congress, that a private National Monument Society was formed to select a designer and to search for funds. Robert Mills's winning design called for a 600-foot-tall decorated obelisk rising from a circular colonnaded building. The building at the base was to be an American pantheon, adorned with statues of national heroes and a massive statue of Washington riding in a chariot pulled by snorting horses.

Because of the marshy conditions of L'Enfant's original site, the position of the monument was shifted to firmer ground 100 yards southeast. (If you walk a few steps north of the monument you can see the stone marker that denotes L'Enfant's original axis.) The cornerstone was laid in 1848 with the same Masonic trowel Washington himself had used to lay the Capitol's cornerstone 55 years earlier. The Monument Society continued to raise funds after construction was begun, soliciting subscriptions of one dollar from citizens across America. It also urged states, organizations, and foreign governments to contribute memorial stones for the construction. Problems arose in 1854, when members of the anti-Papist "Know Nothing" party stole a block donated by Pope Pius IX, smashed it, and dumped its shards into the Potomac. This action, a lack of funds, and the onset of the Civil War kept the monument at a fraction of its final height, open at the top, and vulnerable to the rain. A clearly visible ring about a third of the way up the obelisk testifies to this unfortunate stage of the monument's history. In 1876 Congress finally appropriated $200,000 to finish the monument, and the Army Corps of Engineers took over construction—work was finally completed in December 1884. The Washington Monument is the world's tallest masonry structure. The view from the top takes in most of the District and parts of Maryland and Virginia.

There is usually a wait to take the minute-long elevator ride up the monument's shaft, generally 10 to 15 minutes for each side of the monument that is lined with people. In an effort to do away with the long lines, the Park Service has started using a free timed-ticket system from April through Labor Day. A limited number of tickets are available at the kiosk on 15th St. ⊠ *Constitution Ave. and 15th St. NW,* ☎ *202/426–6840.* ▦ *Free.* ☉ *Apr.–Labor Day, daily 8 AM–midnight; Sept.–Mar., daily 9–5. Metro: Smithsonian.*

The White House Area

In a world full of immediately recognizable images, few are better known—not just in the U.S. but from Chile to China—than the whitewashed, 32-room mansion at 1600 Pennsylvania Avenue, the country's most famous address, known as the White House. The residence of arguably the single most powerful person on the planet, it has an awesome majesty, having been the home of every U.S. president but, ironically, the father of our country, George Washington. This is where the buck stops in America and where the nation turns in times of crisis. After joining the more than 1.5 million people who visit the White House each year, strike out into the surrounding streets to explore the president's neighborhood, which includes some of the oldest houses in the city.

Numbers in the text correspond to numbers in the margin and on the White House Area map.

Sights to See

11 **American Red Cross.** Although it hosts occasional art exhibits, the American Red Cross national headquarters is mainly of passing interest. It's composed of three buildings. The primary building, a neoclassical structure of blinding white marble built in 1917, commemorates the service and devotion of the women who cared for the wounded on both sides during the Civil War. The building's Georgian-style board of governors hall has three stained-glass windows designed by Louis Tiffany. ✉ *430 17th St. NW,* ☎ *202/737–8300.* 🎟 *Free.* 🕘 *Weekdays 9–4. Metro: Farragut West.*

14 **Art Museum of the Americas.** With changing exhibits highlighting 20th-century Latin American artists, this small gallery is in a building that formerly served as the residence for the secretary general of the OAS. ✉ *201 18th St. NW,* ☎ *202/458–6016.* 🎟 *Free.* 🕘 *Tues.–Sat. 10–5. Metro: Farragut West.*

Blair House. A green canopy marks the entrance to Blair House, the residence used by heads of state visiting Washington. Harry S. Truman lived here from 1948 to 1952 while the White House was undergoing its much-needed renovation. A plaque on the fence honors White House policeman Leslie Coffelt, who died in 1950 when Puerto Rican separatists attempted to assassinate President Truman at this site. ✉ *1651 Pennsylvania Ave. Metro: McPherson Square.*

8 **Corcoran Gallery of Art.** The Corcoran is one of the few large museums in Washington outside the Smithsonian family. The beaux arts–style building, its copper roof green with age, was designed by Ernest Flagg and completed in 1897. The gallery's permanent collection numbers more than 11,000 works, including paintings by the first great American portraitists John Copley, Gilbert Stuart, and Rembrandt Peale. The Hudson River School is represented by such works as *Mount Corcoran* by Albert Bierstadt and Frederic Church's *Niagara.* There are also portraits by John Singer Sargent, Thomas Eakins, and Mary Cassatt. European art is seen in the Walker Collection (late-19th- and early 20th-century paintings, including works by Courbet, Monet,

The White House Area

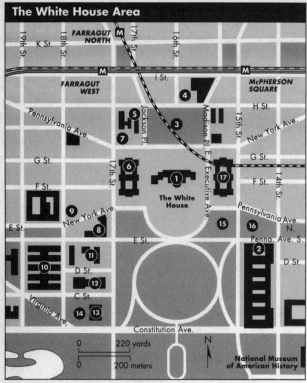

FARRAGUT
NORTH

K St.

19th St.
18th St.
17th St.
16th St.

I St.

FARRAGUT
WEST

McPHERSON
SQUARE

Pennsylvania Ave.

H St.

New York Ave.

Jackson Pl.

Madison Pl.

15th St.

G St.

G St.

F St.

17th St.

The White
House

E. Executive Ave.

14th St.

F St.

New York Ave.

Pennsylvania Ave. N.

E St.

E St.

Penna. Ave. S.

D St.

D St.

C St.

Virginia Ave.

Constitution Ave.

| 0 | 220 yards |
| 0 | 200 meters |

N

National Museum
of American History

American Red
Cross, **11**

Art Museum
of the
Americas, **14**

Corcoran
Gallery of
Art, **8**

Decatur
House, **5**

Department of
the Interior, **10**

House of the
Americas, **13**

Lafayette
Square, **3**

Memorial
Continental
Hall, **12**

Octagon, **9**

Old Executive
Office
Building, **6**

Pershing
Park, **16**

Renwick
Gallery, **7**

St. John's
Episcopal
Church, **4**

Treasury
Building, **17**

White House, **1**

White House
Visitor Center, **2**

William
Tecumseh
Sherman
Monument, **15**

Pissarro, and Renoir) and the Clark Collection (Dutch, Flemish, and French Romantic paintings, and the restored entire 18th-century Grand Salon of the Hotel d'Orsay in Paris). Be sure to see Samuel Morse's *Old House of Representatives* and Hiram Powers's *Greek Slave*, which scandalized Victorian society. Photography and works by contemporary American artists are also among the Corcoran's strengths. ⊠ *17th St. and New York Ave. NW,* ☎ *202/638–1439 or 202/638–3211.* ▣ *Suggested donation: $3.* ☉ *Mon., Wed., and Fri.–Sun. 10–5; Thurs. 10–9; tours of permanent collection Fri.–Wed. at noon, Thurs. at 7:30 PM. Metro: Farragut West.*

NEED A BREAK?

In the Corcoran Gallery the **Café des Artistes** has a lunch menu that includes a selection of salads, light entrées, desserts, and a refreshing assortment of fruit and vegetable shakes. The café also serves a Continental breakfast, an English tea complete with scones and clotted cream, and dinner on Thursday, when the museum is open late. The Sunday brunch, where gospel singers and a jazz band perform live, is very popular.

❺ Decatur House. Designed by Benjamin Latrobe, Decatur House was built for naval hero Stephen Decatur and his wife Susan in 1919. A redbrick, Federal-style building on the corner of H Street and Jackson Place, it was the first private residence on President's Park (the White House doesn't really count as *private*). Decatur had earned the affection of the nation in battles against the British and the Barbary pirates. Planning to start a political career, he used the prize money Congress awarded him for his exploits to build this home near the White House. Tragically, only 14 months after he moved in, Decatur was killed in a duel with James Barron, a disgruntled former Navy officer who held Decatur responsible for his court-martial. Later occupants of the house included Henry Clay, Martin Van Buren, and the Beales, a prominent family from the West whose modifications of the building include a parquet floor showing the state seal of California. The house is now operated by the National Trust. The first floor is furnished as it was in Decatur's time. The second floor is furnished in the Victorian style favored by the Beale family, who owned it until

1956 (thus making Decatur House both the first and *last* private residence on Lafayette Square). ⊠ *748 Jackson Pl. NW,* ☎ *202/842–0920.* ⊠ *$4.* ☉ *Tues.–Fri. 10–3, weekends noon–4; tours on the hr and ½ hr. Metro: Farragut West.*

⑩ Department of the Interior. Designed by Waddy B. Wood, the Department of the Interior building was the most modern government building in the city and the first with escalators and central air-conditioning at the time of its construction in 1937. The outside of the building is somewhat plain, but much of the interior is decorated with paintings that reflect the Interior Department's work. The **Department of the Interior Museum** on the first floor showcases several heroic oil paintings. (You can enter the building at its E Street or C Street doors; adults must show photo ID.) Soon after it opened in 1938, the museum became one of the most popular attractions in Washington; evening hours were maintained even during World War II. The small museum tells the story of the Department of the Interior, a huge agency dubbed the "Mother of Departments" because from it grew the Departments of Agriculture, Labor, Education, and Energy. Today Interior oversees most of the country's federally owned land and natural resources, and exhibits in the museum outline the work done by the Bureau of Land Management, the U.S. Geological Survey, the Bureau of Indian Affairs, the National Park Service, and other Interior branches. Call at least two weeks ahead to schedule a tour of the building's architecture and murals. ⊠ *C and E Sts. between 18th and 19th Sts. NW,* ☎ *202/208–4743.* ⊠ *Free.* ☉ *Weekdays 8–5; closed federal holidays. Metro: Farragut West.*

⑬ House of the Americas. Headquarters of the Organization of American States, House of the Americas contains a cool patio adorned with a pre-Columbian–style fountain and lush tropical plants. This tiny rain forest is a good place to rest when Washington's summer heat is at its most oppressive. The upstairs Hall of Flags and Heroes contains, as the name implies, busts of generals and statesmen from the various OAS member countries as well as each country's flag. ⊠ *17th St. and Constitution Ave. NW,* ☎ *202/458–3000.* ⊠ *Free.* ☉ *Weekdays 9–5:30. Metro: Farragut West.*

❸ Lafayette Square. A lovely park bounded by Pennsylvania Avenue, Madison Place, H Street, and Jackson Place, Layfayette Square is an intimate oasis amid downtown Washington. With such an important resident living across the street, National Capital Park Service gardeners lavish extra attention on the square's trees and flower beds.

When Pierre L'Enfant proposed the location for the Executive Mansion, the only building north of what is today Pennsylvania Avenue was the Pierce family farmhouse, which stood at the northeast corner of the present square. An apple orchard and a family burial ground were the area's two other main features. During the construction of the White House, workers' huts and a brick kiln were set up, and soon private residences began popping up around the square (though sheep would continue to graze on it for years). L'Enfant's original plan for the city designated this area as part of "President's Park"; in essence it was the president's front yard. The egalitarian Thomas Jefferson, concerned that large, landscaped White House grounds would give the wrong impression in a democratic country, ordered that the area be turned into a public park. Soldiers camped in the square during the War of 1812 and the Civil War, turning it at both times into a muddy pit. Today, protesters set their placards up in Lafayette Square, jockeying for positions that face the White House. Although the National Park Service can't restrict the protesters' freedom of speech, it does try to restrict the size of their signs.

NEED A BREAK? Adviser to Woodrow Wilson and other presidents, Bernard Baruch used to eat his lunch in Lafayette Park; you can, too. Nearby, **Loeb's Restaurant** (✉ 15th and I Sts. NW) is a New York–style deli that serves salads and sandwiches to eat there or to go.

⓬ Memorial Continental Hall. A beaux arts building serving as headquarters of the Daughters of the American Revolution, Memorial Continental Hall was the site each year of the DAR's congress until the larger Constitution Hall was built around the corner. An entrance on D Street leads to the **DAR Museum.** Its 50,000-item collection includes fine examples of Colonial and Federal silver, china, porcelain, stoneware, earthenware, and glass. Thirty-three period rooms are decorated in styles representative of various U.S. states, ranging from an 1850 California adobe parlor to a New Hampshire attic filled with toys from the 18th and 19th centuries. Docents are available for tours weekdays 10–2:30. ⊠ *1776 D St. NW,* ☎ *202/879–3240.* 🎟 *Free.* ☉ *Weekdays 8:30–4, Sun. 1–5. Metro: Farragut West.*

❾ **Octagon.** This octagon actually has six, rather than eight, sides. Designed by William Thornton (the Capitol's architect), it was built for John Tayloe III, a wealthy Virginia plantation owner, and was completed in 1801. Thornton chose the unusual shape to conform to the acute angle formed by L'Enfant's intersection of New York Avenue and 18th Street.

After the White House was burned in 1814 the Tayloes invited James and Dolley Madison to stay in the Octagon. It was in a second-floor study that the Treaty of Ghent, ending the War of 1812, was signed. By the late 1800s the building was used as a rooming house. In this century the house served as the headquarters of the American Institute of Architects before the construction of AIA's rather unexceptional building behind it.

A renovation in the 1960s revealed the Octagon's intricate plaster molding and the original 1799 Coade stone mantels (named for the man who invented a now-lost method of casting crushed stone). A far more thorough restoration, completed in 1996, returned the Octagon to its 1815 appearance, topped off by a new, and historically accurate, cypress-shingle roof, complete with balustrade. The galleries inside host changing exhibits on architecture, city planning, and Washington history and design. ⊠ *1799 New York Ave. NW,* ☎ *202/638–3105, TTY 202/638–1538.* 🎟 *$3.* ☉ *Tues.–Fri. 10–4, weekends noon–4. Metro: Farragut West.*

❻ **Old Executive Office Building.** The granite edifice of this building built between 1871 and 1888 may look like a wedding cake (its architect, Alfred B. Mullett, patterned it after the Louvre) but its high ceilings and spacious offices make it popular with occupants, who include members of the executive branch. The Old Executive Office Building has played host to numerous historic events. It was here that Secretary of State Cordell Hull met with Japanese diplomats after the bombing of Pearl Harbor, and it was here that Oliver North and Fawn Hall shredded Iran-Contra documents. ⊠ *Across Pennsylvania Ave. west of White House. Metro: Farragut West.*

⑯ Pershing Park. A quiet sunken garden honors General "Blackjack" Pershing, famed for his failed attempt to capture the Mexican revolutionary Pancho Villa in 1916-1917 and then for commanding the American expeditionary force in World War I, among other military exploits. Engravings on the stone walls recount pivotal campaigns from that war. Ice-skaters glide on the square pool in the winter. ⊠ *15th St. and Pennsylvania Ave. Metro: McPherson Square.*

❼ Renwick Gallery. The Renwick has been at the forefront of the crafts movement, and its collection includes exquisitely designed and made utilitarian items, as well as objects created out of such traditional craft media as fiber and glass. The words "Dedicated to Art" are engraved above the entrance to the French Second Empire–style building, designed by Smithsonian Castle architect James Renwick in 1859 to house the art collection of Washington merchant and banker William Wilson Corcoran. Corcoran was a Southern sympathizer who spent the duration of the Civil War in Europe. While he was away his unfinished building was pressed into service by the government as a quartermaster general's post.

In 1874 the Corcoran, as it was then called, opened as the first private art museum in the city. Corcoran's collection quickly outgrew the building and in 1897 it was moved to a new gallery a few blocks south on 17th Street (described below). After a stint as the U.S. Court of Claims, this building was restored, renamed after its architect, and opened in 1972 as the Smithsonian's museum of American decorative arts. Although crafts were once the poor relations of the art world—handwoven rugs and delicately carved tables were considered somehow less "artistic" than, say, oil paintings and sculptures—they have recently come into their own.

Not everything in the museum is Shaker furniture and enamel jewelry, though. The second-floor Grand Salon is still furnished in the opulent Victorian style Corcoran favored when his collection adorned its walls. Paintings are hung in tiers, one above the other, and in Corcoran's portrait the Renwick itself is visible in the background. ⊠ *Pennsylvania Ave. and 17th St. NW,* ☎ *202/357–2700, TTY 202/357–1729.* ☒ *Free.* ☉ *Daily 10–5:30. Metro: McPherson Square.*

❹ St. John's Episcopal Church. The golden-domed, so-called "Church of the Presidents" sits directly across Lafayette Park from the White House. Every president since Madison has visited the church, and many worshiped here on a regular basis. Built in 1816, the church was the second building on the square. Benjamin Latrobe, who worked on both the Capitol and the White House, designed it in the form of a Greek cross, with a flat dome and a lantern cupola. The church has been altered somewhat since then; later additions include the Doric portico and the cupola tower. You can best sense the intent of Latrobe's design while standing inside under the saucer-shape dome of the original building. Not far from the center of the church is pew 54, where visiting presidents are seated. The kneelers of many of the pews are embroidered with the presidential seal and the names of several chief executives. Brochures are available inside for those who would like to take a self-guided tour. ⊠ *16th and H Sts. NW,* ☎ *202/347–8766.* ☒ *Free.* ☉ *Mon.–Sat. 8–3, tours after 11 AM Sun. service and by appointment. Metro: McPherson Square.*

❼ Treasury Building. Once used as a repository for currency, this is the largest Greek Revival edifice in Washington. Pierre L'Enfant had intended for Pennsylvania Avenue to stretch in a straight, unbroken line from the White House to the Capitol. The plan was ruined by the construction of the Treasury Building on this site just east of the White House. Robert Mills, the architect responsible for the Washington Monument and the Patent Office (now the National Museum of American Art), designed the grand colonnade that stretches down 15th Street. Construction of the Treasury Building started in 1836 and, after several additions, was finally completed in 1869. Guided 90-minute tours are given every Saturday, except holiday weekends, at 10, 10:20, 10:40, and 11, and take visitors past the Andrew Johnson suite, used by Johnson as the executive office while Mrs. Lincoln moved out of the White House; the two-story marble Cash Room; and a 19th-century burglarproof vault lining that saw duty when the Treasury stored currency. Register at least one week ahead for the tour; visitors must provide name, date of birth, and Social Security number and must show a photo ID at the start of the tour. ⊠ *15th St. and Pennsylvania Ave. NW,* ☎ *202/622–0896, TTY 202/622–0692.* ▨ *Free. Metro: McPherson Square.*

....

NEED A BREAK? About one block from the Treasury Building is a glittering urban mall, **The Shops** (⊠ National Press Bldg., F and G Sts. between 13th and 14th Sts. NW), which houses table-service restaurants such as the **Boston Seafood Company,** as well as faster and cheaper fare in its top-floor Food Hall. The luxurious **Old Ebbitt Grill** (⊠ 675 15th St. NW, ☎ 202/347–4800) is a popular watering spot for journalists and television news correspondents. On Mondays, **Benkay** (⊠ 727 15th St. NW, lower level) has an $8 sushi buffet.

....

★ ☾ ❶ **White House.** This "house" surely has the best known address in the U.S.: 1600 Pennsylvania Avenue. Pierre L'Enfant called it the President's House; it was known formally as the Executive Mansion; and in 1902 Congress officially proclaimed it the White House, though, contrary to popular belief, it had been given that nickname even before its white sandstone exterior was painted to cover the fire damage it suffered during the War of 1812. Irishman James Hoban's plan, based on the Georgian design of Leinster Hall near Dublin and of other Irish country houses, was selected in a contest in 1792. The building wasn't ready for its first occupant, John Adams, the second U.S president, until 1800, and so, in a colossal irony, George Washington, who seems to have slept everyplace else, never slept here. Completed in 1829, it has undergone many structural changes since then: Thomas Jefferson, who had entered his own design in the contest under an assumed name, added terraces to the east and west wings. Andrew Jackson installed running water. James Garfield put in the first elevator. Between 1948 and 1952, Harry Truman had the entire structure gutted and restored, adding a second-story porch to the south portico. Each family that has called the White

House home has left its imprint on the 132-room mansion. George Bush installed a horseshoe pit. Most recently, Bill Clinton had a customized jogging track put in.

Tuesday through Saturday mornings (except holidays), from 10 AM to noon, selected public rooms on the ground floor and first floor of the White House are open to visitors. The White House Visitor Center (☞ *below*) disburses tickets March through September; in other months, go directly to the Southeast gate (before 10 AM) or the East gate (after 10 AM), both on East Executive Avenue, between the White House and the Treasury Building. You can write to your representative or senator's office 8–10 weeks in advance of your trip to request special VIP passes for tours between 8 and 10 AM, but these tickets are extremely limited.

You'll enter the White House through the East Wing lobby on the ground floor, walking past the Jacqueline Kennedy Rose Garden. Your first stop is the large white-and-gold **East Room,** the site of presidential news conferences. In 1814 Dolley Madison saved the room's full-length portrait of George Washington from torch-carrying British soldiers by cutting it from its frame, rolling it up, and spiriting it out of the White House. (No fool she, Dolley also rescued her own portrait.) A later occupant, Teddy Roosevelt, allowed his children to ride their pet pony in the East Room.

The Federal-style **Green Room,** named for the moss-green watered silk that covers its walls, is used for informal receptions and "photo opportunities" with foreign heads of state. The president and his guests are often shown on TV sitting in front of the Green Room's English Empire mantel, engaging in what are invariably described as "frank and cordial" discussions. The elliptical **Blue Room,** the most formal space in the White House, is furnished with a gilded Empire-style settee and chairs that were ordered by James Monroe. Another well-known elliptical room, the president's **Oval Office,** is in the semidetached West Wing of the White House, along with other executive offices. The **Red Room** is decorated as an American Empire–style parlor of the early 19th century, with furniture by the New York cabinetmaker Charles-Honoré Lannuier. You'll recognize the marble mantel as the twin of the mantel in the Green Room.

The **State Dining Room,** second in size only to the East Room, can seat 140 guests. The room is dominated by G. P. A. Healy's portrait of Abraham Lincoln, painted after the president's death. The stone mantel is inscribed with a quotation from one of John Adams's letters: "I pray heaven to bestow the best of blessings on this house and all that shall hereafter inhabit it. May none but honest and wise men ever rule under this roof." In Teddy Roosevelt's day a stuffed moose head hung over the mantel. ✉ *1600 Pennsylvania Ave. NW,* ☎ *202/456–7041 or 202/619–7222.* 🎫 *Free.* ⊘ *Tues.–Sat. 10–noon. Metro: McPherson Square.*

❷ White House Visitor Center. If you're visiting the White House during the months of March through September, you need to stop by the visitor center for free tickets. Tickets are dispensed on a first-come, first-served basis. (They are often gone by 9 AM.) Your ticket will show the approximate time of your tour. Also at the center are exhibits pertaining to the White House's construction, its decor, and the families who have lived there. Photographs, artifacts, and videos relate the house's history to those who don't have the opportunity to tour the building personally. ✉ *1450 Pennsylvania Avenue NW, in Commerce Department's Baldrige Hall, E St. between 14th and 15th streets,* ☎ *202/208–1631.* 🎫 *Free.* ⊘ *Daily 7:30–4. Metro: McPherson Square.*

❶⑤ William Tecumseh Sherman Monument. Sherman, whose Atlanta Campaign in 1864 cut a bloody swath of destruction through the Confederacy, was said to be the greatest Civil War general, as the sheer size of this massive monument, set in a small park, would seem to attest. ✉ *Bounded by E and 15th Sts., East Executive Ave., and Alexander Hamilton Pl. Metro: Federal Triangle.*

Capitol Hill

The people who live and work on "the Hill" do so in the shadow of the edifice that lends the neighborhood its name: the gleaming white Capitol building. More than just the center of government, however, the Hill also includes charming residential blocks lined with Victorian row houses and a fine assortment of restaurants, bars, and shops. Capitol

Hill's boundaries are disputed: It's bordered to the west, north, and south by the Capitol, Union Station, and I Street, respectively. Some argue that Capitol Hill extends east to the Anacostia River, others that it ends at 11th Street near Lincoln Park. The neighborhood does in fact seem to grow as members of Capitol Hill's active historic-preservation movement restore more and more 19th-century houses.

Numbers in the text correspond to numbers in the margin and on the Capitol Hill map.

Sights to See

❾ Bartholdi Fountain. Frédéric-Auguste Bartholdi, sculptor of the more famous—and much larger—Statue of Liberty, created this delightful fountain, some 25 feet tall, for the Philadelphia Centennial Exhibition of 1876. The U.S. Government purchased the fountain after the exhibition and placed it on the grounds of the old Botanic Garden on the Mall. It was moved to its present location in 1932. ⊠ *1st St. and Independence Ave. SW. Metro: Federal Center.*

★ **❹ Capitol.** As beautiful as the building itself are the Capitol grounds, landscaped in the late-19th century by Frederick Law Olmsted, Sr., who, along with Calvert Vaux, created New York City's Central Park. On these 68 acres you will find both the tamest squirrels in the city and the highest concentration of television news correspondents, jockeying for a good position in front of the Capitol for their "stand-ups."

When planning the city, Pierre L'Enfant described the gentle rise on which the Capitol sits, known then as Jenkins Hill, as "a pedestal waiting for a monument." The design of this monument was the result of a competition held in 1792; the winner was William Thornton, a physician and amateur architect from the West Indies. With its central rotunda and dome, Thornton's Capitol is reminiscent of Rome's Pantheon, a similarity that must have delighted the nation's founders, who felt the American government was based on the principles of the Republic of Rome.

The cornerstone was laid by George Washington in a Masonic ceremony on September 18, 1793, and in November

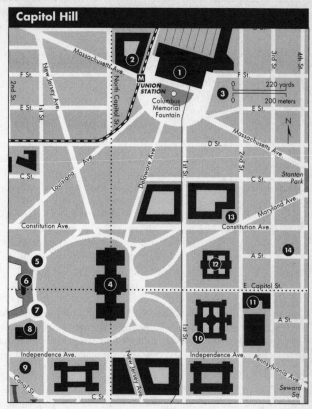

Capitol Hill

Bartholdi
Fountain, **9**

Capitol, **4**

Folger
Shakespeare
Library, **11**

Frederick
Douglass
Townhouse, **14**

Grant
Memorial, **6**

James Garfield
Memorial, **7**

Library of
Congress, **10**

National Postal
Museum, **2**

Peace
Monument, **5**

Sewall-Belmont
House, **13**

Supreme Court
Building, **12**

Thurgood
Marshall
Federal
Judiciary
Building, **3**

Union Station, **1**

United States
Botanic
Gardens, **8**

1800, both the Senate and the House of Representatives moved down from Philadelphia to occupy the first completed section of the Capitol: the boxlike portion between the central rotunda and today's north wing. By 1806 the House wing had been completed, just to the south of what is now the domed center, and a covered wooden walkway joined the two wings.

The Congress House grew slowly and suffered a grave setback on August 24, 1814, when British troops led by Sir George Cockburn marched on Washington and set fire to the Capitol, the White House, and numerous other government buildings. (Cockburn reportedly stood on the House Speaker's chair and asked his men, "Shall this harbor of Yankee democracy be burned?" The question was rhetorical; the building was torched.) The wooden walkway was destroyed and the two wings gutted, but the walls were left standing after a violent rainstorm doused the flames. Fearful that Congress might leave Washington, residents raised money for a hastily built "Brick Capitol" that stood where the Supreme Court is today. Architect Benjamin Henry Latrobe supervised the rebuilding of the Capitol, adding such American touches as the corn-cob-and-tobacco-leaf capitals to columns in the east entrance to the Senate wing. He was followed by Boston-born Charles Bulfinch, and in 1826 the Capitol, its low wooden dome sheathed in copper, was finally finished.

North and south wings were added in the 1850s and '60s to accommodate a growing government trying to keep pace with a growing country. The elongated edifice extended farther north and south than Thornton had planned, and in 1855, to keep the scale correct, work began on a tall cast-iron dome. President Lincoln was criticized for continuing this expensive project while the country was in the throes of the bloody Civil War, but he called the construction "a sign we intend the Union shall go on." This twin-shelled dome, a marvel of 19th-century engineering, rises 285 feet above the ground and weighs 9 million pounds. It expands and contracts up to 4 inches a day, depending on the outside temperature. The figure on top of the dome, often mistaken for Pocahontas, is called *Freedom*.

Guided tours of the Capitol usually start beneath the dome in the Rotunda, but if there's a crowd you may have to wait in a line that forms at the top of the center steps on the east side. If you want to forgo the tour, which is brief but informative, you may look around on your own. Enter through one of the lower doors to the right or left of the main steps. Start your exploration under Constantino Brumidi's *Apotheosis of Washington,* the fresco in the center of the dome. Working as Michelangelo did in the Sistine Chapel, applying paint to wet plaster, Brumidi completed this fresco in 1865. The figures in the inner circle represent the 13 original states of the Union; those in the outer ring symbolize arts, sciences, and industry. The flat, sculpture-style frieze around the rim of the Rotunda depicts 400 years of American history.

Notice the Rotunda's eight immense oil paintings of scenes from American history. The four scenes from the Revolutionary War are by John Trumbull, who served alongside George Washington and painted the first president from life. Twenty-six people have lain in state in the Rotunda, including nine presidents, from Abraham Lincoln to Lyndon Baines Johnson. Underneath the Rotunda, above an empty crypt that was designed to hold the remains of George and Martha Washington, is an exhibit chronicling the construction of the Capitol.

South of the Rotunda is Statuary Hall, once the legislative chamber of the House of Representatives. The room has an interesting architectural feature that maddened early legislators: A slight whisper uttered on one side of the hall can be heard on the other. (Don't be disappointed if this parlor trick doesn't work when you're visiting the Capitol; sometimes the hall is just too noisy.)

To the north, on the Senate side, you can look into the chamber once used by the Supreme Court and into the splendid Old Senate Chamber above it, both of which have been restored. Also be sure to see the Brumidi Corridor on the ground floor of the Senate wing. Frescoes and oil paintings adorn the walls and ceilings, and an intricate, Brumidi-designed bronze stairway leads to the second floor. The Italian artist also memorialized several American heroes, painting them inside trompe l'oeil frames. Trusting that America would continue to produce heroes long after he was gone, Brumidi left some frames empty. The most recent one to be filled, in 1987, honors the crew of the space shuttle *Challenger*.

If you want to watch some of the legislative action in the **House or Senate chambers** while you're on the Hill you'll have to get a gallery pass from the office of your representative or senator. (To find out where those offices are, ask any Capitol police officer, or call 202/224–3121.) In the chambers you'll notice that Democrats sit to the right of the presiding officer, Republicans to the left—the opposite, it's often noted, of their political leanings. *The Washington Post*'s daily "Today in Congress" lists when and where the committees are meeting. ✉ *East end of Mall,* ☎ *202/ 224–3121 or 202/225–6827 (guide service).* 🎟 *Free.* ☉ *Daily 9–4:30; summer hrs determined annually, but Rotunda and Statuary Hall usually open daily 9–8. Metro: Capitol South or Union Station.*

....

NEED A
BREAK?

A meal at a **Capitol cafeteria** may give you a glimpse of a well-known politician or two. A public dining room on the first floor, Senate-side, is open 7:30 AM–3:30 PM. A favorite with legislators is the Senate bean soup, made and served every day since 1901 (no one is sure exactly why, though the menu, which you can take with you, outlines a few popular theories).

....

⑪ Folger Shakespeare Library. The Folger Library's collection of works by and about Shakespeare and his times is second to none. The white-marble Art Deco building, designed by architect Paul Philippe Cret, is decorated with scenes from the Bard's plays. Inside is a reproduction of an inn-yard theater, which is the setting for performances of chamber music, baroque opera, and other events appropriate to the surroundings, and a gallery, designed in the manner of an Elizabethan Great Hall, which hosts rotating exhibits from the library's collection. ✉ *201 E. Capitol St. SE,* ☎ *202/544–4600.* 🎟 *Free.* ☉ *Mon.–Sat. 10–4. Metro: Capitol South.*

⑭ Frederick Douglass Townhouse. No longer open to the public, a gray house with the mansard roof was the first Washington home of the fiery abolitionist and writer. The building once housed the National Museum of African Art, but when the museum moved to new quarters on the Mall (☞ The Mall, *above*) in 1987, the Douglass townhouse was closed. Even though you can't go inside it's worth knowing if you should pass by (it's not far from the Supreme Court building) that here is where one of the seminal figures of the Civil War era once lived. ⊠ *316 A St. Metro: Capitol South.*

⑥ Grant Memorial. The 252-foot-long memorial to the 16th American president and commander in chief of the Union forces during the Civil War is the largest sculpture group in the city. The statue of Ulysses S. Grant on horseback is flanked by Union artillery and cavalry. ⊠ *Near 1st St. and Maryland Ave. SW. Metro: Federal Center.*

⑦ James Garfield Memorial. Near the Grant Memorial and the United States Botanic Gardens is a memorial to the 20th president of the United States. James Garfield was assassinated in 1881 after only a few months in office. Garfield's two primary claims to fame were that he was the last log cabin president, and that his was the second presidential assassination (Lincoln's was first) ending the second-shortest presidency. ⊠ *1st St. and Maryland Ave. SW. Metro: Federal Center.*

⑩ Library of Congress. One of the world's largest libraries, the Library of Congress contains some 108 million items, of which only a quarter are books. The remainder includes manuscripts, prints, films, photographs, sheet music, and the largest collection of maps in the world. Also part of the library is the Congressional Research Service, which, as the name implies, works on special projects for senators and representatives.

Provisions for a library to serve members of Congress were originally made in 1800, when the government set aside $5,000 to purchase and house books that legislators might need to consult. This small collection was housed in the Capitol but was destroyed in 1814, when the British burned the city. Thomas Jefferson, then in retirement at Monticello, offered his personal library as a replacement, noting that "there is, in fact, no subject to which a Member of Congress may not have occasion to refer." Jefferson's collection of 6,487 books, for which Congress eventually paid him $23,950, laid the foundation for the great national library. (Sadly, another fire in 1851 wiped out two-thirds of Jefferson's books.) By the late 1800s it was clear the Capitol building could no longer contain the growing library, and the **Jefferson Building**, the oldest of the three buildings that make up the library, was constructed. The **Adams Building**, on 2nd Street behind the Jefferson, was added in 1939. A third structure, the **James Madison Building**, opened in 1980; it is just south of the Jefferson Building, between Independence Avenue and C Street.

But books are only part of the story. Family trees are explored in the Local History and Genealogy Reading Room. In the Folklife Reading Room, patrons can listen to LP recordings of American Indian music or hear the story of B'rer Rabbit read in the Gullah dialect of Georgia and South Carolina. Items from the library's collection—which includes a Gutenberg Bible—are often on display in the Jefferson and Madison buildings. ⊠ *Jefferson Bldg., 1st St. and Independence Ave. SE,* ☎ *202/707–8000 or 202/707–6400 (taped schedule of general and special reading room hours).* ⊡ *Free.* ☉ *Call for hours open, which change daily. Tours weekdays at 11:30, 1, 2:30, and 4 from Great Hall. Metro: Capitol South.*

NEED A BREAK?

It's easy to grab a bite in the Library of Congress vicinity. The sixth floor dining halls of the **Madison Building** of the library itself offer great views and inexpensive fare. Or head for the library's **Adams Building,** where the south side of Pennsylvania Avenue SE, between Second and Fourth streets, is lined with restaurants and bars frequented by those who live and work on the Hill. Another option is **Le Bon Cafe** (⊠ 210 2nd St. SE), a cozy French bistro serving excellent coffees, pastries, and light lunches.

Memorial to Robert A. Taft. Rising up above the trees in the triangle formed by Louisiana, New Jersey, and Constitution Avenues, a monolithic carillon pays tribute to the son of the 27th president and longtime Republican senator. ⊠ *Constitution and New Jersey Aves. Metro: Union Station.*

❷ **National Postal Museum.** In the newest member of the Smithsonian family of museums, exhibits underscore the important part the mail played in the development of America and include horse-drawn mail coaches, railway mail cars, actual airmail planes, every U.S. stamp issued, many foreign stamps, and a collection of philatelic rarities. The National Museum of Natural History may have the Hope Diamond, but the National Postal Museum has in its collection the container used to mail the priceless gem to the Smithsonian. The museum takes up only a portion of what is the Washington **City Post Office,** designed by Daniel Burnham and completed in 1914. ⊠ *2 Massachusetts Ave. NE,* ☎ *202/357–2700.* ⚏ *Free.* ☉ *Daily 10–5:30. Metro: Union Station.*

❺ **Peace Monument.** A white-marble memorial depicts America in the form of a woman grief-stricken over sailors lost at sea during the Civil War; she is weeping on the shoulder of a second female figure representing History. The plaque inscription refers movingly to navy personnel who "fell in defence of the union and liberty of their country 1861-1865." ⊠ *Traffic circle at 1st St. and Pennsylvania Ave. Metro: Union Station.*

⓭ **Sewall-Belmont House.** This house, the oldest home on Capitol Hill, is now the headquarters of the National Woman's Party. It has a museum that chronicles the early days of the women's movement and is filled with period furniture and portraits and busts of such suffrage-movement leaders as Lucretia Mott, Elizabeth Cady Stanton, and Alice Paul. The redbrick house was built in 1800 by Robert Sewall. Part of the structure dates from the early 1700s, a record for the neighborhood. From 1801 to 1813 Secretary of the Treasury Albert Gallatin lived here. He finalized the details of the Louisiana Purchase in his front-parlor office. The house became the only private residence burned in Washington during the British invasion of 1814, after a resident fired on advancing British troops from an upperstory window. (It was, in fact, the only resistance the British met. The rest of the country was disgusted at Washington's inability to defend itself.) ⊠ *144 Constitution Ave. NE,* ☎ *202/546–3989.* ☞ *Free.* ☉ *Tues.–Fri. 10–3, Sat. noon–4. Metro: Union Station.*

⑫ Supreme Court Building. It wasn't until 1935 that the Supreme Court got its own building: a white-marble temple with twin rows of Corinthian columns designed by Cass Gilbert. In 1800, the justices arrived in Washington along with the rest of the government but were for years shunted around various rooms in the Capitol; for a while they even met in a tavern. William Howard Taft, the only man to serve as both president and chief justice, was instrumental in getting the court a home of its own, though he died before it was completed.

The Supreme Court convenes on the first Monday in October and remains in session until it has heard all of its cases and handed down all its decisions (usually the end of June). On Monday through Wednesday of two weeks in each month, the justices hear oral arguments in the velvet-swathed court chamber. Visitors who want to listen can choose to wait in either of two lines. One, the "three-to-five-minute" line, shuttles visitors through, giving them a quick impression of the court at work. The other line is for those who'd like to stay for the whole show. ⊠ *1st and E. Capitol Sts. NE,* ☎ *202/479–3000.* ☞ *Free.* ☉ *Weekdays 9–4:30. Metro: Capitol South.*

❸ Thurgood Marshall Federal Judiciary Building. If you're in the Union Station neighborhood, the signature work of architect Edward Larabee Barnes is worth taking a moment to pop inside for a look at its spectacular atrium featuring a garden of bamboo five stories tall. ⊠ *Massachusetts Ave. opposite Union Station. Metro: Union Station.*

❶ Union Station. With its 96-foot-high coffered ceiling gilded with eight pounds of gold leaf, the city's train station is one of the Capitol's great spaces and is used for inaugural balls and other festive events. In 1902 the McMillan Commission—charged with suggesting ways to improve the appearance of the city—recommended that the many train lines that sliced through the capital share one main depot. Union Station was opened in 1908 and was the first building completed under the commission's plan. Chicago architect and commission member Daniel H. Burnham patterned the station after the Roman Baths of Diocletian.

For many visitors to Washington, the capital city is first seen framed through the grand station's arched doorways. In its heyday, during World War II, more than 200,000 people swarmed through the station daily. By the '60s, however, the decline in train travel had turned the station into an expensive white-marble elephant. It was briefly, and unsuccessfully, transformed into a visitor center for the Bicentennial; but by 1981 rain was pouring in through the neglected station's roof, and passengers boarded trains at a ramshackle depot behind the station.

The Union Station you see today is the result of a restoration completed in 1988, an effort intended to be the beginning of a revival of Washington's east end. It's hoped that the shops, restaurants, and nine-screen movie theater in Union Station will draw more than just train travelers to the beaux arts building. The jewel of the structure remains its meticulously restored main waiting room. ⊠ *Massachusetts Ave. north of Capitol,* ☎ *202/289–1908. Metro: Union Station.*

NEED A BREAK?   On Union Station's lower level you'll find more than 20 food stalls offering everything from pizza to sushi. There are several restaurants throughout the station, one of the best being **America,** with a menu of regional foods that lives up to its expansive name.

🐾 ⑧ **United States Botanic Gardens.** The rather cold exterior belies the peaceful, plant-filled oasis within. The conservatory includes a cactus house, a fern house, and a subtropical house filled with orchids. Seasonal displays include blooming plants at Easter, chrysanthemums in the fall, and Christmas greens and poinsettias in December and January. Brochures just inside the doorway offer helpful gardening tips. ⊠ *1st St. and Maryland Ave. SW,* ☎ *202/225–8333.* ⊡ *Free.* ☉ *Daily 9–5. Metro: Federal Center SW.*

Old Downtown and Federal Triangle

Just because Washington is a planned city doesn't mean the plan was executed flawlessly. Pierre L'Enfant's design has been alternately shelved and rediscovered several times in the last 200 years. Nowhere have the city's imperfections been more visible than on L'Enfant's grand thoroughfare, Pennsylvania Avenue. By the early '60s it had become a national disgrace, the dilapidated buildings that lined it home to pawn shops and cheap souvenir stores. While riding up Pennsylvania Avenue in his inaugural parade, a disgusted John F. Kennedy is said to have turned to an aide and said, "Fix it!" Washington's downtown—once within the diamond formed by Massachusetts, Louisiana, Pennsylvania, and New York avenues—had its problems, too, many as a result of the riots that rocked the capital in 1968 after the assassination of Martin Luther King, Jr. In their wake, many downtown businesses left the area and moved north of the White House.

In recent years developers have rediscovered "old downtown," and buildings are now being torn down or remodeled at an amazing pace. After several false starts Pennsylvania Avenue is shining once again. This walk explores the old downtown section of the city, then swings around to check the progress on the monumental street that links the Congress House—the Capitol—with the President's House.

Numbers in the text correspond to numbers in the margin and on the Old Downtown and Federal Triangle map.

Sights to See

10 **Department of Commerce.** The western base of Federal Triangle between 14th and 15th streets is the home of the Department of Commerce, charged with promoting U.S. economic development and technological advancement. When it opened in 1932 the Commerce building was the world's largest government office building. It's a good thing there's plenty of space; incongruously, the **National Aquarium** is housed inside. Established in 1873, it's the country's oldest public aquarium, with more than 1,200 fish and other creatures representing 250 species of fresh- and saltwater life on display. A "touch tank" lets you handle more hospitable sea creatures such as crabs and oysters. ⊠ *14th*

St. and Pennsylvania Ave. NW, ☎ *202/482–2825.* 🎟 *$2.*
🕑 *Daily 9–5; sharks fed Mon., Wed., and Sat. at 2; piranhas fed Tues., Thurs., and Sun. at 2. Metro: Federal Triangle.*

⑥ Ford's Theatre. In 1861, Baltimore theater impresario John T. Ford leased the First Baptist Church building that stood on this site and turned it into a successful music hall. The building burned down late in 1862, and Ford rebuilt it. The events of April 14, 1865, would shock the nation and close the theater. On that night, during a production of *Our American Cousin,* John Wilkes Booth entered the presidential box and assassinated Abraham Lincoln. The stricken president was carried across the street to the house of tailor William Petersen. Charles Augustus Leale, a 23-year-old doctor, attended to the president, whose injuries would have left him blind had he ever regained consciousness. To let Lincoln know that someone was nearby, Leale held his hand throughout the night. Lincoln died the next morning.

The federal government bought Ford's Theatre in 1866 for $100,000 and converted it into office space. It was remodeled as a Lincoln museum in 1932 and was restored to its 1865 appearance in 1968. The basement museum contains artifacts such as Booth's pistol and the clothes Lincoln was wearing when he was shot. The theater itself continues to present a complete schedule of plays (☞ The Arts *in* Chapter 5). ✉ *511 10th St. NW,* ☎ *202/426–6924.* 🎟 *Free.* 🕑 *Daily 9–5; theater closed when rehearsals or matinees are in progress (generally Thurs. and weekends); Lincoln Museum in basement remains open at these times. Metro: Metro Center.*

② Friendship Arch. A colorful and ornate 75-foot-wide arch spanning H Street at 7th Street is a reminder of Washington's sister-city relationship with Beijing. *Metro: Gallery Place/Chinatown.*

InterAmerican Development Bank Cultural Center. Founded in 1959, the IADB is an international bank that finances economic and social development in Latin America and the Caribbean. Its small cultural center hosts changing exhibits of paintings, sculptures, and artifacts from member countries. Since it's located across the street from the National Museum of Women in the Arts, which is also worth a visit, you can kill two birds with one stone. ⊠ *1300 New York Ave. NW*, ☎ *202/942–8287.* ▣ *Free.* ☉ *Weekdays 11–6. Metro: Metro Center.*

☙ **⑧ J. Edgar Hoover Federal Bureau of Investigation Building.** The one-hour tour of the FBI building remains one of the most popular tourist activities in the city. A brief film outlines the Bureau's work, while exhibits describe famous past cases and illustrate the FBI's fight against organized crime, terrorism, bank robbery, espionage, extortion, and other criminal activities. There's everything from gangster John Dillinger's death mask to a poster display of the 10 Most Wanted criminals. (Look carefully: Two bad guys were apprehended as a result of tips from tour takers!) You'll also see the laboratories where the FBI painstakingly studies evidence. The high point of the tour comes right at the end: A special agent gives a live-ammo firearms demonstration in the building's indoor shooting range. ⊠ *10th St. and Pennsylvania Ave. NW (tour entrance on E St. NW)*, ☎ *202/324–3447.* ▣ *Free.* ☉ *Tours weekdays 8:45–4:15; closed federal holidays. Metro: Federal Triangle.*

④ Martin Luther King Memorial Library. Designed by Ludwig Miës van der Rohe, one of the founders of modern architecture, this squat black building at 9th and G streets is the largest public library in the city. A mural on the first floor depicts events in the life of the Nobel Prize–winning civil rights activist. Used books are almost always on sale at bargain prices in the library's gift shop. ⊠ *901 G St. NW*, ☎ *202/727–1111.* ▣ *Free.* ☉ *Mon., Wed., and Thurs. 10–7; Tues. 10–9; Fri. and Sat. 10–5:30; Sun. 1–5. Metro: Gallery Place.*

⑨ National Archives. If the Smithsonian Institution is the nation's attic, the Archives, erected in 1935, is the nation's basement, and it bears responsibility for the cataloguing and safekeeping of important government documents and other items. The Declaration of Independence, the Constitution, and the Bill of Rights are on display in the Rotunda of the Archives building, in a case made of bulletproof glass and filled with helium gas to protect the irreplaceable documents. Other objects in the Archives' vast collection include bureaucratic correspondence, veterans and immigration records, treaties, even Richard Nixon's resignation letter and the rifle Lee Harvey Oswald used to assassinate John F. Kennedy. Call at least three weeks in advance to arrange a behind-the-scenes tour (☎ 202/501–5205). ✉ *Constitution Ave. between 7th and 9th Sts. NW,* ☎ *202/501–5000.* 🖼 *Free.* ☉ *Apr.–Labor Day, daily 10–9:30; Sept.–Mar., daily 10–5:30; tour weekdays at 10:15 and 1:15. Metro: Archives/Navy Memorial.*

❸ National Museum of Women in the Arts. Works by prominent female artists from the Renaissance to the present are showcased in this beautifully restored 1907 Renaissance Revival building, one of the larger non-Smithsonian museums, designed by Waddy Wood. Ironically, it was once a men-only Masonic temple. In addition to displaying traveling shows, the museum houses a permanent collection that includes paintings, drawings, sculpture, prints, and photographs by such artists as Georgia O'Keeffe, Mary Cassatt, Élisabeth Vigée-Lebrun, Frida Kahlo, and Judy Chicago. ✉ *1250 New York Ave. NW,* ☎ *202/783–5000.* 🖼 *Suggested donation $3.* ☉ *Mon.–Sat. 10–5, Sun. noon–5. Metro: Metro Center.*

NEED A BREAK?
For a casual lunch in an elegant setting, the café in the **National Museum of Women in the Arts** is just the place.

❺ Old Patent Office Building. Two Smithsonian museums now share the Old Patent Office Building. The **National Portrait Gallery,** with its Civil War photographs, paintings, and prints, presidential portraits, and *Time* magazine covers, is on the south. The **National Museum of American Art,** with displays on early American and western art, is on the north. Construction on the south wing, which was designed by Washington Monument architect Robert Mills, started in 1836. When the huge Greek-Revival quadrangle was completed in 1867 it was the largest building in the country.

During the Civil War, the Patent Office, like many other buildings in the city, was turned into a hospital. Among those caring for the wounded here were Clara Barton and Walt Whitman. In the 1950s the building was threatened with demolition to make way for a parking lot, but the efforts

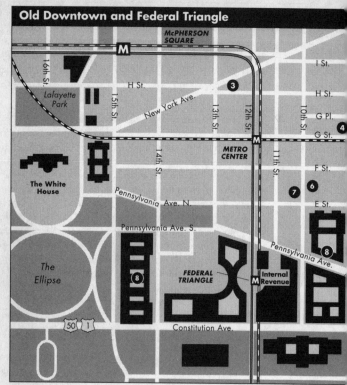

Old Downtown and Federal Triangle

McPHERSON SQUARE

I St.

16th St.

Lafayette Park

H St.

H St.

New York Ave.

15th St.

13th St.

12th St.

G Pl.

10th St.

G St.

METRO CENTER

14th St.

11th St.

F St.

The White House

Pennsylvania Ave. N.

E St.

Pennsylvania Ave. S.

The Ellipse

FEDERAL TRIANGLE

Internal Revenue

Pennsylvania Ave.

50 1

Constitution Ave.

Department of Commerce/ National Aquarium, **10**

Ford's Theatre, **6**

Friendship Arch, **2**

J. Edgar Hoover FBI Building, **8**

Martin Luther King Memorial Library, **4**

National Archives, **9**

National Museum of Women in the Arts, **3**

Old Patent Office Building/ National Museum of American Art and National Portrait Gallery, **5**

Pension Building/ National Building Museum, **1**

Petersen House, **7**

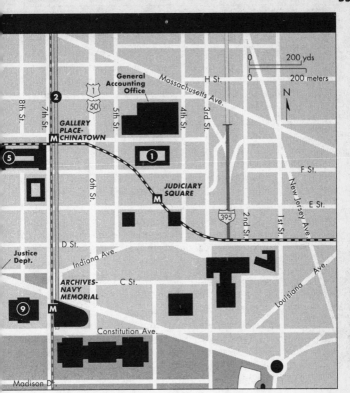

of preservationists saved it. The Smithsonian opened it to the public in 1968.

The first floor of the National Museum of American Art holds displays of early American art and art of the West, as well as a gallery of painted miniatures. Be sure to see *The Throne of the Third Heaven of the Nations' Millennium General Assembly,* by James Hampton. Discarded materials, such as chairs, bottles, and light bulbs, are sheathed in aluminum and gold foil in this strange and moving work of religious art. On the second floor are works by the American Impressionists, including John Henry Twachtman and Childe Hassam. The third floor is filled with modern art, including works by Leon Kroll and Edward Hopper that were commissioned during the '30s by the federal government. The Lincoln Gallery—site of the receiving line at Abraham Lincoln's 1865 inaugural ball—has been restored to its original appearance and contains modern art by Jasper Johns, Robert Rauschenberg, Milton Avery, Kenneth Noland, and others. ⊠ *8th and G Sts. NW,* ☎ *202/357–2700, TTY 202/357–1729.* ◪ *Free.* ◷ *Daily 10–5:30. Metro: Gallery Place.*

You can enter the National Portrait Gallery from any floor of the National Museum of American Art or walk through the courtyard between the two wings. The best place to start a circuit of the Portrait Gallery is on the restored third floor. The mezzanine level of the wonderfully busy room features a **Civil War exhibition,** with portraits, photographs, and lithographs of such wartime personalities as Julia Ward Howe, Frederick Douglass, Ulysses S. Grant, and Robert E. Lee. There are also life casts of Abraham Lincoln's hands and face. Highlights of the Portrait Gallery's second floor include the **Hall of Presidents** (featuring a portrait or sculpture of each chief executive) and the George Washington "Lansdowne" portrait. The first floor features portraits of well-known American athletes and performers. *Time* magazine gave the museum its collection of Person of the Year covers and many other photos and paintings that the magazine has commissioned over the years. Parts of this collection are periodically on display. ⊠ *8th and F Sts. NW,* ☎ *202/357–2700, TTY 202/357–1729.* ◪ *Free.* ◷ *Daily 10–5:30. Metro: Gallery Place.*

NEED A
BREAK?

The **Patent Pending** restaurant, between the two museums, serves an ample selection of salads, sandwiches, hot entrées, and other treats. Tables and chairs in the large museum courtyard make sitting outside enjoyable when the weather is pleasant.

❶ **Pension Building.** The open interior of this mammoth red-brick edifice is one of the city's great spaces and has been the site of inaugural balls for more than 100 years. (The first ball was for Grover Cleveland in 1885; because the building wasn't finished at the time, a temporary wooden roof and floor were erected.) The eight central Corinthian columns are the largest in the world, rising to a height of 75 feet.

The building was erected between 1882 and 1887 to house workers who processed the pension claims of veterans and their survivors, an activity that intensified after the Civil War. The architect was U.S. Army Corps of Engineers General Montgomery C. Meigs, who took as his inspiration the Italian Renaissance–style Palazzo Farnese in Rome. The Pension Building now houses the **National Building Museum,** devoted to architecture and the building arts. "Washington: Symbol and City" is a permanent exhibit that outlines the capital's architectural history, from monumental core to residential neighborhoods. Recent temporary exhibits have explored the rebuilding of Oklahoma City and the dome as a symbol of American democracy. ⊠ *F St. between 4th and 5th Sts. NW,* ☎ *202/272–2448.* 🎟 *Free.* ☉ *Mon.–Sat. 10–4, Sun. noon–4; tour weekdays at 12:30, weekends at 12:30 and 1:30. Metro: Judiciary Square.*

❼ **Petersen House.** Lincoln died in the house of William Petersen, a tailor, on the morning after being shot. You can see the restored front and back parlors of the house, as well as the bedroom where the president died. Most of the furnishings are not original, but the pillow and bloodstained pillowcases are those used on that fateful night. ⊠ *516 10th St. NW,* ☎ *202/426–6830.* 🎟 *Free.* ☉ *Daily 9–5. Metro: Metro Center.*

Georgetown

The area that would come to be known as George (after George II), then George Towne and, finally, Georgetown, was part of Maryland when it was settled in the early 1700s by Scottish immigrants, many of whom were attracted to the region's tolerant religious climate. Long before the District of Columbia was formed, Georgetown, Washington's oldest neighborhood, was a separate city that boasted a harbor full of ships and warehouses filled with tobacco. Georgetown's position at the farthest point up the Potomac one could reach by boat made it an ideal transit-and-inspection point for farmers who grew tobacco in Maryland's interior. In 1789 the state granted the town a charter, but two years later Georgetown—along with Alexandria, its counterpart in Virginia—was included by George Washington in the Territory of Columbia, site of the new capital.

While Washington struggled, Georgetown thrived. Wealthy traders built their mansions on the hills overlooking the river; merchants and the working class lived in more modest homes closer to the water's edge. (When Georgetowners thought the dismal capital was dragging them down, they asked to be given back to Maryland, the way Alexandria was given back to Virginia in 1845.) Tobacco eventually became a less important commodity, and Georgetown became a milling center, using water power from the Potomac. When the Chesapeake & Ohio (C&O) Canal was completed in 1850, the city intensified its milling operations and became the eastern end of a waterway that stretched 184 miles to the west.

Although Georgetown today is synonymous with affluence, for most of its history it was a working–class city, and the original names of its streets—Water Street, The Keys, Fishing Lane—attest to the past importance of traditional trades like fishing to the region's economy. Georgetown's rich history and success instilled in citizens of all colors feelings of superiority that many feel linger today—the neighborhood's historic preservationists are among the most vocal in the city.

Washington has filled in around Georgetown over the years, but the former tobacco port retains an air of aloofness. Its narrow streets, which refuse to conform to Pierre L'Enfant's plan for the Federal City, make up the capital's wealthiest neighborhood and are the nucleus of its nightlife. The lack of a Metro station in Georgetown means you'll have to take a bus or walk to this part of Washington. It's about a 15-minute walk from the Dupont Circle or Foggy Bottom Metro station. (If you'd rather take a bus, the G2 Georgetown University bus goes from Dupont Circle west along P Street. The 34 and 36 Friendship Heights buses leave from 22nd and Pennsylvania and deposit you at 31st and M.)

Numbers in the text correspond to numbers in the margin and on the Georgetown map.

Sights to See

☾ **C&O Canal.** This waterway kept Georgetown open to shipping after its harbor had filled with silt. George Washington was one of the first to advance the idea of a canal linking the Potomac with the Ohio River across the Appalachians. Work started on the C&O Canal in 1828, and when it opened in 1850, its 74 locks linked Georgetown with Cumberland, Maryland, 184 miles to the northwest (still short of its intended destination). Lumber, coal, iron, wheat, and flour moved up and down the canal, but it was never as successful as its planners had hoped it would be. Many of the bridges spanning the canal in Georgetown were too low to allow anything other than fully loaded barges to pass underneath, and competition from the Baltimore & Ohio Railroad eventually spelled an end to profitability. Today the canal is a part of the National Park system, and walkers follow the towpath once used by mules while canoeists paddle the canal's calm waters. ⊠ *1057 Thomas Jefferson St. NW,* ☎ *202/653–5190, 301/299–2026; group reservations and rates, 301/299–3613.* ⊡ *$5.* ☉ *90-min barge trip mid-Apr.–early Nov., Wed.–Sun. at 11, 1, and 3.*

❻ **Cox's Row.** To get a representative taste of the Federal and Victorian houses in the area, walk along the 3300 block of N Street. The group of five Federal houses between 3339 and 3327 N Street is known collectively as Cox's Row, after John Cox, a former mayor of Georgetown, who built them in 1817. The flat-front, redbrick Federal house at **3307 N Street** was the home of then-Senator John F. Kennedy and his family before the White House beckoned.

⑩ Dumbarton House. Its symmetry and the two curved wings on the north side make Dumbarton, built around 1800, a distinctive example of Georgian architecture. The man who built the house, Joseph Nourse, was registrar of the U.S. Treasury. Dolley Madison is said to have stopped here when fleeing Washington in 1814. Today it serves as the headquarters of the National Society of the Colonial Dames of America.

Eight rooms inside Dumbarton House have been restored to Colonial splendor, with period furnishings such as mahogany American Chippendale chairs, hallmark silver, Persian rugs, and a breakfront cabinet filled with rare books. Other notable items include a 1789 Charles Willson Peale portrait of Benjamin Stoddert's children (with an early view of Georgetown harbor in the background), Martha Washington's traveling cloak, and a British redcoat's red coat. Group tours may be arranged by appointment. ⊠ *2715 Q St. NW,* ☎ *202/337–2288.* ☒ *Suggested donation $3.* ☉ *Tues.–Sat. 10–12:15.*

⑧ Dumbarton Oaks. Don't confuse Dumbarton Oaks with the nearby Dumbarton House. In 1944 one of the most important events of the 20th century took place in Dumbarton Oaks, when representatives of the United States, Great Britain, China, and the Soviet Union met in the music room here to lay the groundwork for the United Nations.

Career diplomat Robert Woods Bliss and his wife Mildred bought the property in 1920 and set about taming the sprawling grounds and removing 19th-century additions that had marred the Federal lines of the 1801 mansion. In 1940 the Blisses conveyed the estate to Harvard University, which maintains world-renowned collections of Byzantine and pre-Columbian art there.

If you have even a mild interest in flowers, shrubs, trees, and magnificent natural beauty, you'll enjoy a visit to Dumbarton Oaks's 10 acres of formal gardens, one of the loveliest spots in all of Washington (enter via R Street). A full-time crew of a dozen gardeners toils to maintain the stunning collection of terraces, geometric gardens, tree-shaded brick walks, fountains, arbors, and pools. ⊠ *Art collections, 1703 32nd St. NW,* ☎ *202/339–6401 or 202/342–3200;*

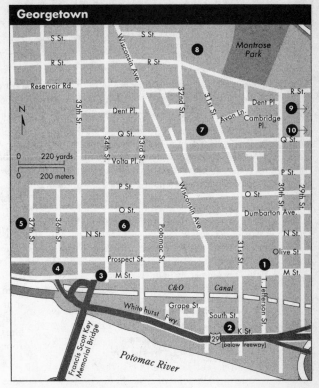

Georgetown

Cox's Row, **6**

Dumbarton House, **10**

Dumbarton Oaks, **8**

Evermay, **9**

Exorcist steps, **4**

Francis Scott Key Memorial Park, **3**

Georgetown University, **5**

Old Stone House, **1**

Suter's Tavern, **2**

Tudor Place, **7**

gardens, ✉ *31st and R Sts. NW.* ▨ *Art collections, suggested donation $1; gardens Apr.–Oct. $3, Nov.–Mar. free.* ☉ *Art collections Tues.–Sun. 2–5; gardens Apr.–Oct., daily 2–6; Nov.–Mar., daily 2–5; both closed national holidays and Dec. 24.*

⑨ Evermay. A Georgian manor house built around 1800 by real estate speculator Samuel Davidson, Evermay is almost hidden by its black-and-gold gates and high brick wall. Davidson wanted it that way. He sometimes took out advertisements in newspapers warning sightseers to avoid his estate "as they would a den of devils or rattlesnakes." The mansion is in private hands, but its grounds are often opened for garden tours. ✉ *1623 28th St. NW.*

④ *The Exorcist* Steps. The heights of Georgetown to the north above N Street contrast with the busy jumble of the old waterfront. To reach the higher ground you can walk up M Street past the old brick streetcar barn at Number 3600 (now a block of offices), turn right, and climb the 75 steps that figured prominently in the eerie movie *The Exorcist.* If you prefer a less demanding climb, walk up 34th Street instead.

③ Francis Scott Key Memorial Park. A small noisy park near Key Bridge (a house owned by Key was demolished in 1947 to make room for its contstruction) honors the Washington attorney who "by the dawn's early light" penned the national anthem, upon seeing that the flag had survived the night's British bombardment of Ft. McHenry in Baltimore harbor during the War of 1812. ✉ *M St. between 34th St. and Key Bridge.*

Georgetown Estates. Georgetown's largest and grandest estates occupy the northern part of the neighborhood, commanding fine views of Rock Creek to the east and of the Potomac River below. Once you're in Georgetown, the best way to get to the estates is to walk north either on Wisconsin Avenue (the bustling commercial route) or a block east, on 31st Street (a quieter residential street), depending on your mood. Strolling 31st Street will give you a chance to admire more of the city's finest houses.

⑤ Georgetown University. Founded in 1789 by John Carroll, first American bishop and first archbishop of Baltimore,

Georgetown is the oldest Jesuit school in the country. About 12,000 students attend Georgetown, known now as much for its perennially successful basketball team as for its fine programs in law, medicine, and the liberal arts. When seen from the Potomac or from Washington's high ground, the Gothic spires of Georgetown's older buildings give the university an almost medieval look. ⊠ *37th and O Sts.*

❶ Old Stone House. Here's the Capitol's oldest window into the past. Work on this fieldstone house, thought to be Washington's only surviving pre-Revolutionary building, was begun in 1764 by a cabinetmaker named Christopher Layman. The house, now a museum, was used as both a residence and a place of business by a succession of occupants. Five of the house's rooms are furnished with the simple sturdy artifacts—plain tables, spinning wheels, etc.—of 18th-century middle-class life. The National Park Service maintains the house and its lovely gardens in the rear, which are planted with fruit trees and perennials. ⊠ *3051 M St. NW,* ☎ *202/426–6851.* 🎟 *Free.* ☉ *Memorial Day–Labor Day, daily 9–5; Labor Day–Memorial Day, Wed.–Sun. 9–5; closed major holidays.*

❷ Suter's Tavern. Peer through a vine-covered fence at a vacant lot to see a **plaque** commemorating Suter's Tavern. In March 1791, in the one-story hostelry that stood on this spot, George Washington met with the men who owned the tobacco farms and swampy marshes to the east of Georgetown and persuaded them to sell their land to the government so construction of the District of Columbia could begin. ⊠ *31st and K Sts.*

❼ Tudor Place. Stop at Q Street between 31st and 32nd streets, look through the trees to the north, at the top of a sloping lawn, and you'll see the neoclassical Tudor Place, designed by Capitol architect William Thornton and completed in 1816. On a house tour you'll see chairs that belonged to George Washington, Francis Scott Key's desk, and spurs of members of the Peter family who were killed in the Civil War (although the house was in Washington, the family was true to its Virginia roots and fought for Dixie). The grounds contain many specimens planted in the early 19th century. The house was built for Thomas Peter, son of Georgetown's first mayor, and his wife, Martha Custis, Martha Washington's granddaughter. It was because of this connection to the president's family that Tudor Place came to house many items from Mount Vernon. The yellow stucco house is interesting for its architecture—especially the dramatic, two-story domed portico on the south side—but its familial heritage is even more remarkable: Tudor Place stayed in the same family for 178 years, until 1983, when Armistead Peter III died. Before his death, Peter established a foundation to restore the house and open it to the public. Tour reservations are advised. ⊠ *1644 31st St. NW,* ☎ *202/965–0400.* 🖃 *Suggested donation $6.* ☉ *Tour Tues.–Fri. at 10, 11:30, 1, and 2:30; Sat. hourly 10–4 (last tour at 3); garden spring and fall, Sun. noon–4.*

Dupont Circle

Three of Washington's main thoroughfares intersect at Dupont Circle: Connecticut, New Hampshire, and Massachusetts avenues. With a handsome small park and a splashing fountain in the center, Dupont Circle is more than a deserted island around which traffic flows, making it an exception among Washington circles. The activity on the circle spills over into the surrounding streets, one of the liveliest, most vibrant neighborhoods in Washington.

Development near Dupont Circle started during the post–Civil War boom of the 1870s. As the city increased in stature, the nation's wealthy and influential citizens began building their mansions near the circle. The area underwent a different kind of transformation in the middle of this century, when the middle and upper classes deserted Washington for the suburbs, and in the '60s the circle became the starting point for rowdy, litter-strewn marches sponsored by various counterculture groups. Today the neighborhood is once again fashionable, and its many restaurants, offbeat shops, and specialty bookstores lend it a distinctive, cosmopolitan air. Stores and clubs catering to the neighborhood's large gay community are abundant.

Numbers in the text correspond to numbers in the margin and on the Dupont Circle and Foggy Bottom map.

Sights to See

❸ **Bison Bridge.** Tour guides at the Smithsonian's Museum of Natural History are quick to remind visitors that America never had buffalo; the big shaggy animals that roamed the plains were bison. (True buffalo are African and Asian animals of the same family.) Though many maps and guidebooks call this the Buffalo Bridge, the four bronze statues by A. Phimister Proctor are of bison. Officially called the **Dumbarton Bridge**, the structure stretches across Rock Creek Park into Georgetown. Its sides are decorated with busts of Native Americans, the work of architect Glenn Brown, who, along with his son Bedford, designed the bridge in 1914. The best way to see the busts is to walk the footpath along Rock Creek or to lean over the green railings beside the bison and peer through the trees. ⊠ *23rd and Q Sts. NW. Metro: Dupont Circle.*

❽ **B'nai B'rith Klutznick Museum.** Devoted to the history of the Jewish people, this museum's permanent exhibits span 20 centuries and highlight Jewish festivals and the rituals employed to mark the various stages of life. A wide variety of Jewish decorative art is on display. Changing exhibits highlight the work of contemporary Jewish artists. ⊠ *1640 Rhode Island Ave. NW,* ☎ *202/857–6583.* ☞ *Suggested donation $2.* ☉ *Sun.–Fri. 10–5; closed federal and Jewish holidays. Metro: Dupont Circle or Farragut North.*

❶ **Dupont Circle.** Originally known as Pacific Circle, this hub was the westernmost circle in Pierre L'Enfant's original design for the Federal City. The name was changed in 1884, when Congress authorized construction of a bronze statue honoring Civil War hero Admiral Samuel F. Dupont. The statue fell into disrepair, and Dupont's family—who had never liked it anyway—replaced it in 1921 with the fountain you see today. The marble fountain, with its allegorical figures Sea, Stars, and Wind, was created by Daniel Chester French, the sculptor of Lincoln's statue in the Lincoln Memorial.

As you look around the circumference of the circle, you'll be able to see the special constraints within which architects in Washington must work. Since a half-dozen streets converge on Dupont Circle, the buildings around it are, for the most part, wedge shaped and set on oddly shaped plots

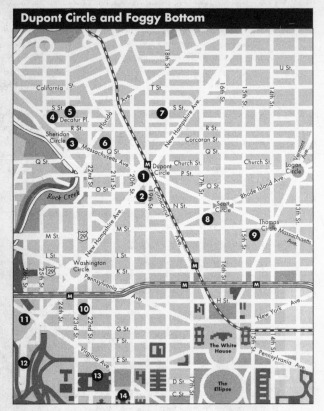

Dupont Circle and Foggy Bottom

Bison Bridge, **3**

B'nai B'rith
Klutznick
Museum, **8**

Department
of State
Building, **13**

Dupont
Circle, **1**

Federal
Reserve
Building, **14**

George
Washington
University, **10**

Heurich
Mansion/
Historical
Society of
Washington,
D.C., **2**

John F.
Kennedy
Center for the
Performing
Arts, **12**

National
Geographic
Society, **9**

National
Museum of
American
Jewish Military
History, **7**

Phillips
Collection, **6**

Textile
Museum, **5**

Watergate, **11**

Woodrow
Wilson
House, **4**

of land like massive slices of pie. Only two of the great houses that stood on the circle in the early 20th century remain today. The Renaissance-style house at **15 Dupont Circle**, next to P Street, was built in 1903 for Robert W. Patterson, publisher of the *Washington Times-Herald*. The **Sulgrave Club,** at the corner of Massachusetts Avenue, was also once a private home and is now likewise a club. Neither is open to the public. *Metro: Dupont Circle.*

NEED A
BREAK?

Connecticut Avenue near Dupont Circle is chockablock with restaurants. The **Chesapeake Bagel Bakery** (⊠ 1636 Connecticut Ave. NW) is a low-key lunchroom that serves a wide variety of bagel sandwiches. At **Kramerbooks** (⊠ 1517 Connecticut Ave. NW), relax over dinner or a drink after browsing the volumes on display. One of the best Chinese restaurants in the city, **City Lights of China** (⊠ 1731 Connecticut Ave. NW) serves Cantonese, Sichuan, and Mandarin dishes. Specialties include Peking duck, whole fish steamed with ginger, and eggplant in garlic sauce.

Fondo Del Sol Visual Art and Media Center. A nonprofit center devoted to the cultural heritage of the Americas, the Fondo Del Sol Visual Art and Media Center offers changing exhibitions covering contemporary, pre-Columbian, and folk art. The center also offers a program of lectures, concerts, poetry readings, exhibit tours, and an annual summer festival featuring salsa and reggae music. ⊠ *2112 R St. NW,* ☎ *202/483–2777.* ☞ *About $3.* ☉ *Wed.–Sat. 12:30–5. Metro: Dupont Circle.*

➋ **Heurich Mansion.** Currently housing the **Historical Society of Washington, D.C.,** the Heurich Mansion is a severe Romanesque Revival building that was the home of Christian Heurich, a German orphan who made his fortune in this country in the beer business. After Heurich's widow died, in 1955, the house was turned over to the Historical Society and today is its headquarters and houses its voluminous archives. All the furnishings were owned and used by the Heurichs, making the interior of the house an eclectic Victorian treasure trove of plaster detailing, carved wooden doors, and painted ceilings. Docents who give tours of the house are adept at answering questions about other Washington landmarks, too. ⊠ *1307 New Hampshire Ave. NW,* ☎ *202/785–2068.* ☜ *45-min house tour $3.* ☉ *Wed.–Sat. 10–4; tour Wed.–Sat. at noon, 1, 2, and 3. Metro: Dupont Circle.*

🖐 ❾ **National Geographic Society.** Founded in 1888, the society is best known for its yellow-border magazine, found in doctor's offices, family rooms, and attics across the country. The society has sponsored numerous expeditions throughout its 100-year history, including those of Admirals Peary and Byrd and underwater explorer Jacques Cousteau. **Explorers Hall,** entered from 17th Street, is the magazine come to life. Recently renovated, Explorers Hall invites visitors to learn about the world in a decidedly interactive way. You can experience everything from a mini-tornado to video "touch-screens" that explain various geographic concepts and then quiz you on what you've learned. The most dramatic events take place in Earth Station One, a 72-seat amphitheater that sends the audience on a journey around the world. The centerpiece is a hand-painted globe, 11 feet in diameter, that floats and spins on a cushion of air, showing off different features of the planet. ⊠ *17th and M Sts.,* ☎ *202/857–7588; group tours, 202/857–7689.* ☜ *Free.* ☉ *Mon.–Sat. and holidays 9–5, Sun. 10–5. Metro: Farragut North.*

❼ **National Museum of American Jewish Military History.** The museum's focus is on American Jews as being first and foremost American citizens who have served in every war the nation has fought. On display are their weapons, uniforms, medals, recruitment posters, and other military memorabilia. The few specifically religious items—a camouflage yarmulke, rabbinical supplies fashioned from shell casings and parachute silk—underscore the strange demands placed on religion during war. ⊠ *1811 R St. NW,* ☎ *202/265–6280.* ☜ *Free.* ☉ *Weekdays 9–5, Sun. 1–5; closed federal and Jewish holidays. Metro: Dupont Circle.*

❻ **Phillips Collection.** The first permanent museum of modern art in the country, the masterpiece-filled Phillips Collection is unique both in origin and content. In 1918 Duncan Phillips, grandson of a founder of the Jones and Laughlin Steel Company, started to collect art for a museum that

It helps to be pushy in airports.

Introducing the revolutionary new TransPorter™ from American Tourister® It's the first suitcase you can push around without a fight. TransPorter's™ exclusive four-wheel design lets you push it in front of you with almost no effort–the wheels take the weight. Or pull it on two wheels if you choose. You can even stack on other bags and use it like a luggage cart.

Stable 4-wheel design.

TransPorter™ is designed like a dresser, with built-in shelves to organize your belongings. Or collapse the shelves and pack it like a traditional suitcase. Inside, there's a suiter feature to help keep suits and dresses from wrinkling. When push comes to shove, you can't beat a TransPorter™ For more information on how you can be this pushy, call 1-800-542-1300.

Shelves collapse on command.

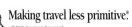

Making travel less primitive.®

©1996 American Tourister®

Use your MCI Card for the easy way to call when traveling.

MCI ⭐ Calling Card

415 555 1234 2244
J.D. SMITH

Convenience on the road

- Your MCI Card® number is your home number, guaranteed.
- Pre-programmed to speed dial to your home.
- Call from any phone in the U.S.

MCI ⭐

1 - 8 0 0 - 7 5 4 - 8 9 4 1

http://www.mci.com

would stand as a memorial to his father and brother, who had died within 13 months of each other. Three years later what was first called the Phillips Memorial Gallery opened in two rooms of this Georgian-Revival home near Dupont Circle.

Not interested in a painting's market value or its faddishness, Phillips searched for works that impressed him as outstanding products of a particular artist's unique vision. Holdings include works by Georges Braque, Paul Cézanne, Paul Klee, Henri Matisse, John Henry Twachtman, and the largest museum collection in the country of the work of Pierre Bonnard. The exhibits change regularly. The collection's best-known paintings include Renoir's *Luncheon of the Boating Party, Repentant Peter* by both Goya and El Greco, *A Bowl of Plums* by 18th-century artist Jean-Baptiste Siméon Chardin, Degas's *Dancers at the Bar,* Van Gogh's *Entrance to the Public Garden at Arles,* and Cézanne's self-portrait, the painting Phillips said he would save first if his gallery caught fire.

Works of a favorite artist are often grouped together in "exhibition units," and, unlike most other galleries (where uniformed guards appear uninterested in the masterpieces around them), the Phillips employs students of art, many of whom are artists themselves, to sit by the paintings and answer questions. ⊠ *1600 21st St. NW,* ☎ *202/387–2151.* ✏ *$6.50, Thurs. night $5.* ☉ *Tues., Wed., Fri., and Sat. 10–5; Thurs. 10–8:30; Sun. noon–7; tour Wed. and Sat. at 2; gallery talks 1st and 3rd Thurs. of month at 12:30. Metro: Dupont Circle.*

❺ Textile Museum. In the 1890s, founder George Hewitt Myers purchased his first Oriental rug for his dorm room at Yale and subsequently collected more than 12,000 textiles and 1,500 carpets. An heir to the Bristol-Myers fortune, Myers and his wife lived two houses down from Woodrow Wilson, at 2310 S Street, in a home designed by John Russell Pope, architect of the National Archives and Jefferson Memorial. Myers bought the Waddy Wood-designed house next door, at Number 2320, and opened his museum to the public in 1925. Rotating exhibits are taken from a permanent collection of historic and ethnographic items that include Coptic and pre-Columbian textiles, Kashmir embroidery, and Turkman tribal rugs. At least one show of modern textiles—such as quilts or fiber art—is mounted each year. ⊠ *2320 S St. NW,* ☎ *202/667–0441.* 🖅 *Suggested donation $5.* 𝄇 *Mon.–Sat. 10–5, Sun. 1–5; closed major holidays; highlight tour Sept.–May, Wed. and weekends at 2. Metro: Dupont Circle.*

❹ **Woodrow Wilson House.** Wilson is the only president who stayed in Washington after leaving the White House. (He's also the only president buried in the city, inside the Washington Cathedral.) He and his second wife, Edith Bolling Wilson, retired in 1920 to this Georgian Revival house designed by Washington architect Waddy B. Wood. (Wood also designed the Department of the Interior Building on C Street and the National Museum of Women in the Arts building.) The house had been built in 1915 for a carpet magnate, and on the first and third floors you can still see the half-snaps that run along the edges of the floors to hold down the long-gone wall-to-wall carpeting.

President Wilson suffered a stroke toward the end of his second term, in 1919, and he lived out the last few years of his life on this quiet street. Edith made sure he was comfortable; she had a bed constructed that was the same dimensions as the large Lincoln bed Wilson had slept in while in the White House. She also had the house's trunk lift electrified so the partially paralyzed president could move from floor to floor. When the streetcars stopped running in 1962 the elevator stopped working. It had received its electricity directly from the streetcar line.

Wilson died in 1924. Edith survived him by 37 years. After she died in 1961, the house and its contents were bequeathed to the National Trust for Historic Preservation. On view inside are such items as a Gobelins tapestry, a baseball signed by King George V, and the shell casing from the first shot fired by U.S. forces in World War I. The house also contains memorabilia related to the history of the short-lived League of Nations, including the colorful flag Wilson hoped would be adopted by that organization. ⊠ *2340 S St. NW,* ☎ *202/387–4062.* 🖅 *$5.* 𝄇 *Tues.–Sun. 10–4; closed major holidays. Metro: Dupont Circle.*

Foggy Bottom

The Foggy Bottom area of Washington—bordered roughly by the Potomac and Rock Creek to the west, 20th Street to the east, Pennsylvania Avenue to the north, and Constitution Avenue to the south—has three main claims to fame: the State Department, the Kennedy Center, and George Washington University. In 1763 a German immigrant named Jacob Funk purchased this land, and a community called Funkstown sprang up on the Potomac. This nickname is only slightly less amusing than the present one, an appellation that is derived from the wharves, breweries, lime kilns, and glassworks that were near the water. Smoke from these factories combined with the swampy air of the low-lying ground to produce a permanent fog along the waterfront.

The smoke-belching factories ensured work for the hundreds of German and Irish immigrants who settled in Foggy Bottom in the 19th century. By the 1930s, however, industry was on the way out, and Foggy Bottom had become a poor, predominantly black part of Washington. The opening of the State Department headquarters in 1947 reawakened middle-class interest in the neighborhood's modest row houses. Many of them are now gone, and Foggy Bottom today suffers from a split personality, and tiny, one-room-wide row houses sit next to large, mixed-use developments.

Sights to See

⑬ Department of State building. The foreign policy of the United States is formulated and administered by battalions of brainy analysts in the huge State Department building, which also serves as the headquarters of the United States Diplomatic Corps. All is presided over by the Secretary of State, who is fourth in line for the presidency (after the Vice President, Speaker of the House, and president *pro tempore* of the Senate) should the president be unable to serve. On the top floor are the opulent **Diplomatic Reception Rooms,** decorated in the manner of great halls of Europe and the rooms of Colonial American plantations. The museum-quality furnishings include a Philadelphia highboy, a Paul Revere bowl, and the desk on which the Treaty of Paris was signed. The largest room boasts a specially loomed carpet so heavy and large it had to be airlifted in by helicopter.

The rooms are used 15–20 times a week to entertain foreign diplomats and heads of state; you can see them, too, but you need to register for a tour well in advance of your visit. Summer tours must be booked up to three months in advance. ⊠ *23rd and C Sts. NW,* ☎ *202/647–3241, TTY 202/736–4474.* 🎫 *Free.* ☉ *Tour weekdays at 9:30, 10:30, and 2:45. Metro: Foggy Bottom.*

⑭ Federal Reserve Building. Whether or not interest rates are raised or lowered in an attempt to control the economy gets decided in this imposing marble edifice, its bronze entryway topped by a massive eagle. Designed by Folger Library architect Paul Cret, "the Fed" is on Constitution Avenue between 21st and 20th streets. It seems to say, "Your money's safe with us." Even so, there isn't any money here. Ft. Knox and New York's Federal Reserve Bank hold most of the Federal Reserve System's gold. The stolid building is a bit more human inside, with a varied collection of art and four special art exhibitions every year. A 45-minute tour includes a film that attempts to explain exactly what it is that "the Fed" does. Call 202/452–2526 to arrange a tour. ⊠ *Enter on C St. between 20th and 21st Sts.,* ☎ *202/452–3686.* 🎫 *Free.* ☉ *Weekdays 9:30–2, tour Thurs. at 2:30. Metro: Foggy Bottom.*

⑩ George Washington University. George Washington had always hoped the capital would be home to a world-class university. He even left 50 shares of stock in the Patowmack Canal Co. to endow it. Congress never acted upon his wishes, however, and it wasn't until 1822 that the university that would eventually be named after the first president began to take shape. The private Columbian College in the District of Columbia opened that year with the aim of training students for the Baptist ministry. In 1904 the university shed its Baptist connections and changed its name to George Washington University. In 1912 it moved to its present location and since that time has become the second largest landholder in the District (after the federal government). Students have ranged from J. Edgar Hoover to Jacqueline Kennedy Onassis. In addition to modern university buildings GWU occupies many 19th-century houses. The downtown campus covers much of Foggy Bottom south of Pennsylvania Avenue between 19th and 24th streets. *Metro: Foggy Bottom.*

⑫ John F. Kennedy Center for the Performing Arts. Prior to 1971, Washington after dark was primarily known for cocktail parties, not culture. The opening of the Kennedy Center in that year instantly established the Capitol as a cultural mecca on an international scale. Concerts, ballets, opera, musicals, and drama are presented in the center's five theaters, and movies are screened almost every night in the theater of the American Film Institute.

The idea for a national cultural center had been proposed by President Eisenhower in 1958. John F. Kennedy had also strongly supported the idea, and after his assassination it was decided to dedicate the center to him as a living memorial. The Grand Foyer, lighted by 18 1-ton Orrefors crystal chandeliers, is 630 feet long. (Even at this size it is mobbed at intermission.) Many of the center's furnishings were donated by foreign countries: The chandeliers came from Sweden, the Matisse tapestries outside the Opera House came from France, and the 3,700 tons of white Carrara marble for the interior and exterior of the building were a gift from Italy. Flags fly in the Hall of Nations and the Hall of States, and in the center of the foyer is a 7-foot-high bronze **bust of Kennedy** by sculptor Robert Berks.

The Friends of the Kennedy Center maintain a **Performing Arts Library** on the roof terrace level, mounting periodic theatrical and musical exhibits (original Mozart manuscripts were a recent offering). ⊠ *New Hampshire Ave. and Rock Creek Pkwy. NW,* ☎ *202/467–4600; tour information, 202/416–8341; Performing Arts Library, 202/707–8780.* ☞ *Free.* ☉ *Daily 10–9 (or until last show lets out); box office Mon.–Sat. 10–9, Sun. and holidays noon–9; tour daily 10–1; Performing Arts Library Tues.–Sat. noon–8. Metro: Foggy Bottom.*

NEED A
BREAK?

There are two restaurants on the top floor of the Kennedy Center. The **Roof Terrace Restaurant** is the more expensive, with a lunch menu that offers open-face sandwiches and salads. The **Encore Café** has soups, chili, salads, and hot entrées starting at under $5.

⑪ Watergate. Thanks to the events that took place on the night of June 17, 1972, the Watergate is possibly the world's most notorious apartment-office complex. As Nixon aides E. Howard Hunt, Jr., and G. Gordon Liddy sat in the Howard Johnson Motor Lodge across the street, five of their men were caught trying to bug the Democratic National Committee, headquartered on the sixth floor of the building, in an attempt to subvert the democratic process on behalf of the then president of the United States. A marketing company occupies the space today.

The suffix "-gate" is attached to any political scandal nowadays, but the Watergate itself was named after a monumental flight of steps that lead down to the Potomac behind the Lincoln Memorial.

Even before the break-in, the Watergate—which first opened in 1965—was well known in the Capitol. Within its distinctive curving lines and behind its "toothpick" balusters have lived some of Washington's most famous—and infamous— citizens, including attorney general John Mitchell and presidential secretary Rose Mary Woods of Nixon White House fame, and such power brokers as Jacob Javits, Alan Cranston, and Bob and Elizabeth Dole. The embassies of Qatar, the United Arab Emirates, Sweden, and Yemen are also in the Watergate. ✉ *2600 Virginia Ave. Metro: Foggy Bottom.*

Alexandria

Just a short Metro ride away from Washington, Old Town Alexandria today attracts visitors seeking a break from the monuments and hustle-and-bustle of the District and interested in an encounter with America's Colonial heritage. Founded in 1749 by Scottish merchants eager to capitalize on the booming tobacco trade, Alexandria emerged as one of the most important ports in Colonial America. The city's history is linked to the most significant events and personages of the Colonial and Revolutionary periods. This colorful past is still alive in restored 18th- and 19th-century homes, churches, and taverns; on the cobbled streets; and on the revitalized waterfront, where clipper ships dock and artisans display their wares.

The quickest way to get to Old Town is to take the Metro to the King Street stop (about 25 minutes from Metro Center). If you're driving you can take either the George Washington Memorial Parkway or Jefferson Davis Highway (Route 1) south from Arlington.

Numbers in the text correspond to numbers in the margin and on the Old Town Alexandria map.

Sights to See

⑪ **Alexandria Black History Resource Center.** The history of African Americans in Alexandria and Virginia from 1749 to the present is recounted here. Alexandria's history is hardly limited to the families of George Washington and Robert E. Lee. The federal census of 1790 recorded 52 free blacks living in the city, and the port town was one of the largest slave exportation points in the South, with at least two bustling slave markets. ⊠ *638 N. Alfred St.,* ☎ *703/838-4356.* 🖙 *Free.* ⊙ *Tues.–Sat. 10–4.*

④ **Athenaeum.** One of the most noteworthy structures in Alexandria, the Athenaeum is a striking, reddish-brown Greek Revival edifice at the corner of Prince and Lee streets. It was built as a bank in the 1850s. ⊠ *201 Prince St.*

⑩ **Boyhood home of Robert E. Lee.** The childhood home in Alexandria of the commander in chief of the Confederate forces during the Civil War is a fine example of a 19th-century town house with Federal architecture and antique furnishings and paintings. ⊠ *607 Oronoco St.,* ☎ *703/548-8454.* 🖙 *$3.* ⊙ *Mon.–Sat. 10–4, Sun. 1–4; closed Dec. 15–Feb. 1 except on Sun. closest to Jan. 19 for Lee's birthday celebration; occasionally closed weekends for private events.*

⑤ **Captain's Row.** Many of Alexandria's sea captains built their homes on the block of Prince Street between Lee and Union, hence the name. The cobblestones in the street were allegedly laid by Hessian mercenaries who had fought for the British during the Revolution and were held in Alexandria as prisoners of war.

⑦ **Carlyle House.** The grandest of Alexandria's older houses, Carlyle House was patterned after a Scottish country manor house. The structure was completed in 1753 by Scottish mer-

76

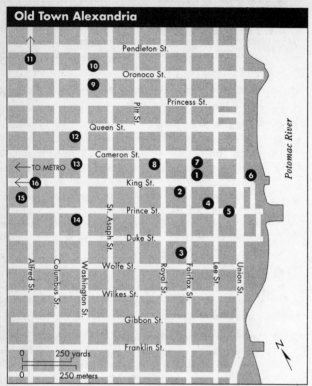

Old Town Alexandria

Pendleton St.

Oronoco St.

Princess St.

Queen St.

Cameron St.

← TO METRO

King St.

Prince St.

Duke St.

Wolfe St.

Wilkes St.

Gibbon St.

Franklin St.

Pitt St.

St. Asaph St.

Alfred St.

Columbus St.

Washington St.

Royal St.

Fairfax St.

Lee St.

Union St.

Potomac River

0   250 yards
0   250 meters

Alexandria Black History Resource Center, **11**

Athenaeum, **4**

Boyhood home of Robert E. Lee, **10**

Captain's Row, **5**

Carlyle House, **7**

Christ Church, **13**

Friendship Fire House, **15**

Gadsby's Tavern Museum, **8**

George Washington Masonic National Memorial, **16**

Lee Corner, **9**

Lloyd House, **12**

Lyceum, **14**

Old Presbyterian Meeting House, **3**

Ramsey House, **1**

Stabler-Leadbeater Apothecary, **2**

Torpedo Factory Arts Center, **6**

chant John Carlyle. This was General Braddock's headquarters and the place where he met with five royal governors in 1755 to plan the strategy and funding of the
early campaigns of the French and Indian War. ⊠ *121 N.
Fairfax St.,* ☎ *703/549–2997.* ☑ *$3.* ☉ *Tues.–Sat. 10–
4:30, Sun. noon–4:40; tour every ½ hr.*

⑬ Christ Church. Both Washington and Lee were pewholders
here. (Washington paid 36 pounds and 10 shillings—a lot
of money in those days—for Pew 60.) Built in 1773, Christ
Church is a fine example of an English Georgian country-
style church. It has a fine Palladian window, an interior balcony, and a wrought-brass-and-crystal chandelier brought
from England at Washington's expense. ⊠ *118 N. Washington St.,* ☎ *703/549–1450.* ☑ *Free.* ☉ *Weekdays 9–4,
Sat. 9–4, Sun. 2–4:30; occasionally closed weekends for
private events.*

Confederate Statue. In 1861, when Alexandria was occu-
pied by Union forces, the 800 soldiers of the city's garri-
son marched out of town to join the Confederate Army. In
the middle of Washington and Prince streets stands the
Confederate Statue marking the point at which they as-
sembled. In 1885 Confederate veterans proposed a memorial to honor their fallen comrades. This statue, based on
John A. Elder's painting *Appomattox,* is of a lone soldier
glumly surveying the battlefields after General Robert E.
Lee's surrender. The names of 100 Alexandria Confederate dead are carved on the base.

⑮ Friendship Fire House. Alexandria's showcase firehouse is
outfitted like a typical 19th-century firehouse. ⊠ *107 S. Alfred St.,* ☎ *703/838–3891.* ☑ *Suggested donation $1.* ☉
Fri. and Sat. 10–4, Sun. 1–4.

⑧ Gadsby's Tavern Museum. Gadsby's Tavern Museum is
housed in the old City Tavern and Hotel, which was a center of political and social life in the late 18th century.
George Washington attended birthday celebrations in the
ballroom here. A tour of the facilities takes you through
the taproom, game room, assembly room, ballroom, and
communal bedrooms. ⊠ *134 N. Royal St.,* ☎ *703/838–
4242.* ☑ *$3.* ☉ *Oct.–Mar., Tues.–Sat. 11–4, Sun. 1–4 (last*

tour 3:15); Apr.–Sept., Tues.–Sat. 10–5, Sun. 1–5 (last tour 4:15); tour 15 mins before and 15 mins after the hr.

⑯ George Washington Masonic National Memorial. Since Alexandria, like Washington, has no really tall buildings, the spire of the George Washington Masonic National Memorial dominates the surroundings and is visible for miles. The building fronts King Street, one of Alexandria's major east-west arteries; from the 9th floor observation deck visitors get a spectacular view of Alexandria, with Washington in the distance. The building contains furnishings from the first Masonic lodge in Alexandria, in which George Washington was a member; he became a Mason in 1852 and was a Worshipful Master, a high rank, at the same time he served as president. ⊠ *101 Callahan Dr.,* ☎ *703/683–2007.* ▢ *Free.* ☉ *Daily 9–5; 50-min guided tour of building and observation deck daily at 9:30, 10:30, 11:30, 1, 2, 3, and 4.*

⑨ Lee Corner. The corner of Alexandria's Washington and Oronoco streets is known as Lee Corner because at one time a Lee-owned house stood on each of the four corners. Two survive. One is the **Lee-Fendall House,** the home of several illustrious members of the Lee family, including Richard Henry Lee, signer of the Declaration of Independence, and cavalry commander Henry "Light Horse Harry" Lee. ⊠ *614 Oronoco St.,* ☎ *703/548–1789.* ▢ *$3.* ☉ *Tues.–Sat. 10–4, Sun. noon–4; occasionally closed weekends for private events.*

⑫ Lloyd House. A fine example of Georgian architecture, Lloyd House, built in 1797, is now operated as part of the Alexandria Library and houses a collection of rare books and documents relating to city and state history. ⊠ *220 N. Washington St.,* ☎ *703/838–4577.* ▢ *Free.* ☉ *Mon.–Sat. 9–5.*

⑭ Lyceum. Built in 1839, the Lyceum served alternately as the Alexandria Library, a Civil War hospital, a residence, and an office building. It was restored in the 1970s and now houses two art galleries and a museum devoted to the area's history. A limited amount of travel information for the entire state is also available here. ⊠ *201 S. Washington St.,* ☎ *703/838–4994.* ▢ *Free.* ☉ *Mon.–Sat. 10–5, Sun. noon–5.*

❸ **Old Presbyterian Meetinghouse.** Built in 1774, the Old Presbyterian Meetinghouse was, as its name suggests, more than a church. It was a gathering place in Alexandria vital to Scottish patriots during the Revolution. Eulogies for George Washington were delivered here on December 29, 1799. In a corner of the churchyard you'll find the **Tomb of the Unknown Soldier of the American Revolution.** ⊠ *321 S. Fairfax St.,* ☎ *703/549–6670.* ☞ *Free.* ☉ *Sanctuary weekdays 9–5 (if locked, obtain key from church office at 316 S. Royal St.).*

❶ **Ramsay House.** The best place to start a tour of Alexandria's Old Town is at the **Alexandria Convention & Visitors Bureau,** in Ramsay House, the home of the town's first postmaster and lord mayor, William Ramsay. The structure is believed to be the oldest house in Alexandria. Ramsay was a Scotsman, as a swatch of his tartan on the door proclaims. Travel counselors here provide information, brochures, and self-guided walking tours of the town. Visitors are given a 24-hour permit that allows them to park free at any two-hour metered spot. ⊠ *221 King St., 22314,* ☎ *703/838–4200, TTY 703/838–6494.* ☉ *Daily 9–5.*

❷ **Stabler-Leadbeater Apothecary.** Once patronized by George Washington and the Lee family, Alexandria's Stabler-Leadbeater Apothecary is the second-oldest apothecary in the country. It was here, on October 17, 1859, that Lt. Col. Robert E. Lee received orders to move to Harper's Ferry to suppress John Brown's insurrection. The shop now houses a small museum of 18th-century apothecary memorabilia, including one of the finest collections of apothecary bottles in the country (some 800 bottles in all). ⊠ *105–107 S. Fairfax St.,* ☎ *703/836–3713.* ☞ *$2.* ☉ *Mon.–Sat. 10–4, Sun. 1–5.*

❻ **Torpedo Factory Arts Center.** A former munitions plant (naval torpedoes were actually manufactured here during World War I and World War II), now converted into studios and galleries for some 175 professional artists and artisans, the Torpedo Factory Arts Center is one of Alexandria's most popular attractions. Almost every imaginable medium is represented, from printmaking and sculpture to jewelry making, pottery, and stained glass. Visitors can view the workshops, and most of the art and crafts are for sale at reasonable prices. ✉ *105 N. Union St.,* ☎ *703/838–4565.* ⊠ *Free.* ⊙ *Daily 10–5.*

The Torpedo Factory complex also houses the **Alexandria Archaeology Program,** a city-operated research facility devoted to urban archaeology and conservation. Artifacts from excavations dug in Alexandria are on display. ✉ *105 N. Union St.,* ☎ *703/838–4399.* ⊠ *Free.* ⊙ *Tues.–Fri. 10–3, Sat. 10–5, Sun. 1–5.*

Around Washington

The city and environs of Washington (including parts of Maryland and Virginia) are dotted with worthwhile attractions that are outside the range of the walks presented in this chapter. You may find some intriguing enough to go a little out of your way to visit.

Anacostia Museum. The richness of African-American culture is on display in the Anacostia museum, a Smithsonian museum in Southeast Washington's historic Anacostia neighborhood. Past exhibits have covered black inventors and aviators, the influential role of black churches, the history of the civil rights movement, African-American life in the antebellum South, and the beauty of African-American quilts. ✉ *1901 Fort Pl. SE,* ☎ *202/287–3369.* ⊠ *Free.* ⊙ *Daily 10–5. Metro: Navy Yard.*

Arlington National Cemetery. Some 250,000 American war dead, as well as many notable Americans (among them Presidents William Howard Taft and John F. Kennedy, General John Pershing, and Admiral Robert E. Peary) are interred in these 612 acres across the Potomac River from Washington, established as the nation's cemetery in 1864. While you are at Arlington you will probably hear the clear, doleful sound of a trumpet playing taps or the sharp reports of a gun salute. Approximately 15 funerals are held here daily. It is projected the cemetery will be filled in 2020. Although not the largest cemetery in the country, Arlington is certainly the best known, a place where visitors can trace America's history through the aftermath of its battles.

To get there, you can take the Metro, travel on a Tourmobile bus, or walk across Memorial Bridge from the District (southwest of the Lincoln Memorial). If you're driving, there's a large paid parking lot at the skylit **visitor center** on Memorial Drive. Stop at the center for a free brochure with a detailed map of the cemetery. (If you're looking for a specific grave, the staff will consult microfilm records and give you directions on how to find it. You should know the deceased's full name and, if possible, his or her branch of service and year of death.) ☎ 703/697–2131. ▱ *Free.* ☉ *Apr.–Sept., daily 8–7; Oct.–Mar., daily 8–5.*

Bethune Museum and Archives. Mary McLeod Bethune founded Florida's Bethune-Cookman College, established the National Council of Negro Women, and served as an adviser to President Franklin D. Roosevelt. Exhibits in the museum named after her focus on the achievements of black women. The museum also hosts concerts, lectures, and films throughout the year. ✉ *1318 Vermont Ave. NW,* ☎ *202/332–1233.* ▱ *Free.* ☉ *Weekdays 10–4. Metro: McPherson Square.*

Franciscan Monastery and Gardens. Not far from the **National Shrine of the Immaculate Conception** (☞ *below*), the Byzantine-style Franciscan Monastery contains facsimiles of such Holy Land shrines as the Grotto of Bethlehem and the Holy Sepulcher. Underground are reproductions of the catacombs of Rome. The gardens are especially beautiful, planted with roses that bloom in the summer. ✉ *14th and Quincy Sts. NE,* ☎ *202/526–6800.* ▱ *Donation requested.* ☉ *Daily 9–5; catacombs tour on the hr (except noon) Mon.–Sat. 9–4, Sun. 1–4. Metro: Brookland–Catholic University.*

Frederick Douglass National Historic Site. Cedar Hill, the Anacostia home of noted abolitionist Frederick Douglass, was the first place designated by Congress as a Black National Historic Site. Douglass, an ex-slave who delivered fiery abolitionist speeches at home and abroad, resided here from 1877 until his death in 1895. The house has a wonderful view of the Federal City across the Anacostia River and contains many of Douglass's personal belongings. A short film on Douglass's life is shown at a nearby visitor center. ✉ *1411*

W St. SE, ☎ *202/426–5961.* 🎫 *Free.* ☉ *Mid-Oct.–mid-Apr.,
daily 9–4 (last tour 3); mid-Apr.–mid-Oct., daily 9–5 (last
tour 4); tour on the hr. Metro: Anacostia, then Bus B2.*

Hillwood Museum. Hillwood House, cereal heiress Marjorie
Merriweather Post's 40-room Georgian mansion in Washington, contains a large collection of 18th- and 19th-cen-
tury French and Russian decorative art that includes gold
and silver work, icons, lace, tapestries, china, and Fabergé
eggs. Also on the estate are a dacha filled with Russian objects and an Adirondacks-style cabin that houses an assortment of Native American artifacts. The grounds are
composed of lawns, formal French and Japanese gardens,
and paths that wind through plantings of azaleas, laurels,
and rhododendrons. Make reservations for the house tour
well in advance. ✉ *4155 Linnean Ave. NW,* ☎ *202/686–
5807.* 🎫 *House and grounds $10; grounds only $2.* ☉
*House tour Mar.–Jan., Tues.–Sat. 9:30–3; grounds
Mar.–Jan., Tues.–Sat. 9–5. Metro: Van Ness/UDC.*

National Shrine of the Immaculate Conception. The largest
Catholic church in the United States, the National Shrine
of the Immaculate Conception was begun in 1920 and
built with funds contributed by every parish in the country. Dedicated in 1959, the shrine is a blend of Romanesque
and Byzantine styles, with a bell tower that reminds many
of St. Mark's in Venice. ✉ *Michigan Ave. and 4th St. NE,*
☎ *202/526–8300.* ☉ *Apr.–Oct., daily 7–7; Nov.–Mar., daily
7–6; Sat. vigil mass at 5:15; Sun. mass at 7:30, 9, 10:30,
noon, 1:30 (in Latin), and 4:30. Metro: Brookland–Catholic
University.*

☫ **National Zoological Park.** Part of the Smithsonian Institution, the National Zoo is one of the foremost zoos in the
world. Created by an Act of Congress in 1889, the 163-
acre zoological park was designed by landscape architect
Frederick Law Olmsted, the man who designed the U.S.
Capitol grounds. For years the zoo's most famous residents
were giant pandas Hsing-Hsing and Ling-Ling, gifts from
China in 1972. But female Ling-Ling died of heart failure
in 1993 at age 23. Hsing-Hsing is now the only giant panda
in the United States.

The zoo has had success with numerous other species, however, including red pandas, Pere David's deer, golden lion tamarins, and pygmy hippopotamuses. The only Komodo dragons in the country are at the National Zoo. Innovative compounds show many animals in naturalistic settings, including the Great Flight Cage—a walk-in aviary in which birds fly unrestricted. Giant crabs, octopuses, cuttlefish, and worms are displayed in an invertebrate exhibit. Zoolab, the Reptile Discovery Center, and the Bird Resource Center all offer activities that teach young visitors about biology. The most ambitious addition to the zoo is Amazonia, a reproduction of a South American rain forest ecosystem. Also new to the zoo is the Cheetah Conservation Area, a grassy compound that's home to a family of the world's fastest cats. ⊠ *3000 block of Connecticut Ave. NW,* ☎ *202/673–4800 or 202/673–4717.* 🖼 *Free.* ☉ *Apr. 15–Oct. 15, grounds daily 8–8, animal buildings daily 9–6, Amazonia daily 10–4; Oct. 16– Apr. 14, grounds daily 8–6, animal buildings daily 9–4:30, Amazonia daily 10–4:30. Metro: Cleveland Park or Woodley Park/Zoo.*

Pentagon. To call the colossal edifice that serves as headquarters of the United States Department of Defense "mammoth" is an understatement. This is, quite simply, the largest office building in the world. Actually the Pentagon is not one but five concentric buildings, collectively as wide as three Washington Monuments laid end to end, that cover a vast 34 acres. The buildings are connected by 17½ miles of corridors through which 23,000 military and civilian personnel pass each day. There are 691 drinking fountains, 7,754 windows, and a blizzard of other eye-popping statistics. Astonishingly, all this was completed in 1943 after just two years of construction.

The escalator from the Pentagon Metro station surfaces right into the gargantuan office building. The 75-minute tour of the Pentagon takes you past only those areas that are meant to be seen by outside visitors. In other words, you won't see situation rooms, communications centers, or gigantic maps outlining U.S. and foreign troop strengths. A uniformed serviceman or -woman (who conducts the entire tour walking backward, lest anyone slip away down a corridor) will take you past hallways lined with the portraits of past and present military leaders, scale models of Air Force planes and Navy ships, and the Hall of Heroes, where the names of all the Congressional Medal of Honor winners are inscribed. Occasionally you will catch a glimpse through an interior window of the Pentagon's 5-acre interior courtyard. In the center—at ground zero—is a hot dog stand. A photo ID is required for admission. ⊠ *Off I–395, Arlington, VA,* ☎ *703/695–1776.* ☑ *Free.* ☉ *Tour weekdays every ½ hr 9:30–3:30; closed federal holidays.*

Sasakawa Peace Foundation. A little art gallery in D.C.'s downtown business district, the Sasakawa Peace Foundation is bankrolled by a Japanese industrialist whose stated aim is to increase understanding between the United States and Japan. Contemporary Japanese and American artists show such work as ceramics, enamels, sculpture, and photographs. Visitors can also browse through a library of Japanese literature. Free videotapes on Japanese life are shown Thursday from noon to 2. ⊠ *1819 L St. NW,* ☎ *202/296–6694.* ☑ *Free.* ☉ *Weekdays 10–6. Metro: Farragut North.*

☙ **Washington Dolls' House and Toy Museum.** A collection of American and imported dolls, dollhouses, toys, and games, most from the Victorian period, fills a compact museum, founded in 1975 by a dollhouse historian. Miniature accessories, dollhouse kits, and antique toys and games are on sale in the museum's shops. ⊠ *5236 44th St. NW,* ☎ *202/244–0024.* ☑ *$3.* ☉ *Tues.–Sat. 10–5, Sun. noon–5. Metro: Friendship Heights.*

3 Dining

By
Deborah
Papier

Updated
by Holly
Bass

AS THE NATION'S CAPITAL, Washington finds itself playing host to an international array of visitors and newcomers. This constant infusion of new cultures means that District restaurants are getting better and better. (And sometimes, cheaper and cheaper: The sluggish economy of the early '90s has meant more reasonably priced fare and fixed-price specials in many of the city's top dining rooms.) Despite the dearth of ethnic neighborhoods and the kinds of restaurant districts found in many cities, you *can* find almost any type of food here, from Nepalese to Salvadoran to Ethiopian. Even the French-trained chefs who have traditionally set the standard in fine dining are turning to health-conscious New American cuisine, spicy Southwestern recipes, or bite-size appetizers called *tapas* for new inspiration.

In the city's one officially recognized ethnic enclave, **Chinatown** (centered on G and H streets NW between 6th and 8th, with its own Metro station at Gallery Place), Burmese, Thai, and other Asian cuisines are adding new variety to the area's many traditional Chinese restaurants. The latter entice visitors with huge brightly lit signs and offer such staples as beef with broccoli or kung pao chicken in a spicy sauce with roasted peanuts. But discriminating diners will find far better food at the smaller, less obvious restaurants. A good rule of thumb is to look for recent reviews in the *Washingtonian Magazine, Washington Post,* and *Washington Times,* which proud owners display on doors or in windows.

Aside from Chinatown, there are seven areas of the city where restaurants are concentrated:

Most of the deluxe restaurants are **downtown** near K Street NW, also the location of many of the city's blue-chip law firms. These are the restaurants that feed off expense-account diners and provide the most elegant atmosphere, most attentive service, and often the best food. In the **old downtown district,** visitors with children can take advantage of the many sandwich shops geared to office workers to grab a quick bite during the day but will find far fewer choices evenings and weekends. However, the entire downtown area is in a state of flux gastronomically, with famed restaurants like Jean-Louis in the Watergate closing their doors and new ones blossoming. Trendy microbrewery/ restaurants and cigar lounges are part of the new wave.

Another popular restaurant district is **Georgetown,** whose central intersection is Wisconsin Avenue and M Street. Here are some of the city's priciest houses as well as some of its cheesiest businesses, and its restaurants are similarly diverse, with white-tablecloth dining places next door to hole-in-the-wall joints. The closest Metro stop for all Georgetown restaurants is Foggy Bottom; the walk can still be substantial—15–20 minutes—depending on the place. Consult the Georgetown map before you set out. Restaurants in the adjacent **West End** are worth checking out as well. This area, bounded roughly by Rock Creek Park to the west, N Street to the north, 20th Street to the east, and K Street to the south, is increasingly bridging the gap between Georgetown and downtown restaurant zones.

An exuberantly diverse culinary competitor to Georgetown is **Adams-Morgan.** Eighteenth Street NW extending south from Columbia Road is wall-to-wall restaurants, with new ones opening so fast it's almost impossible to track them. Although the area has retained some of its Hispanic identity, the new eating establishments tend to be Asian, New American (traditional American ingredients given a French turn), Ethiopian, and Caribbean. Parking can be impossible on weekends. The nearest Metro stop—Woodley Park/Zoo—is a 10- to 15-minute walk; while it's a safe stroll at night, it may be more convenient to take a cab. **Woodley Park** has culinary temptations of its own, with a lineup of popular ethnic restaurants right by the Metro.

Just down the hill from 18th Street the **U Street** corridor begins. In the 1930s and 1940s this was the place to enjoy a late night drink and hear jazz greats like Duke Ellington, Billie Holliday, and Charlie Parker; they came to Washington from New York's Harlem district, then a nationally famous center of culture and the arts. After decades of neglect and devastation from the '60s riots, the U Street area has recently undergone a revitalization campaign. With some of the hippest bars in the District, quirky vintage stores, and numerous cafés, the neighborhood draws a young adult crowd day and night. U Street is home to several small clubs where DJs or live bands—playing everything from punk rock to rap to acid jazz (a fusion of jazz and danceable hiphop beats)—appear almost every night. Restaurants stay open late on weekend nights and offer good food at low prices, everything from burgers to gourmet pizza to Ethiopian dishes (eateries serving this African country's cuisine are abundant in the Capitol, and popular). The U Street vicinity is known for excellent fried fish spots like the Big Fish Deli and Webb's Southern Food; unfortunately they don't offer seating. Free parking is available after 8 PM in the Reeves Center Building on the corner of 14th and U streets.

South from U Street and north from K Street is **Dupont Circle,** around which a number of restaurants are clustered. Some of the city's best white-tablecloth restaurants serving Italian food can be found here. You'll find a variety of cafés, most with outdoor seating. The District's better gay-friendly establishments are here as well. Chains like Starbuck's and Hannibal's have put fancy coffee on every corner, but long-established espresso bars, like the 24-hour Afterwords (located within a bookstore), are a good source for breakfast and light or late fare. Those on 17th Street NW are especially popular with young adults.

Capitol Hill has a number of bar-eateries that cater to Congressional types in need of fortification after a day spent running the country. The dining possibilities on Capitol Hill are boosted by Union Station, which contains some decent—if pricey—restaurants. There's also a large food court with fast food ranging from barbecue to sushi.

The restaurants in many of the city's luxury hotels are another source of fine dining. The Willard Hotel's formal dining room, the Mayflower's Nicholas, the Ritz-Carlton's Jockey Club, and the Morrison-Clark Inn's dining room are especially noteworthy. The cuisine is often artful and fresh, with special care given to ingredients, preparation, and presentation. Of course, such attention to detail comes at a price. One less expensive way to experience these nationally recognized restaurants is a weekday lunch (☞ Chapter 5).

CATEGORY	COST*
$$$$	over $35
$$$	$25–$35
$$	$15–$25
$	under $15

per person for a three-course meal, excluding drinks, service, and sales tax (10% in D.C., 4.5%–9% in VA, 5% in MD)

What to Wear

Gentlemen may be more comfortable wearing jackets and/or ties in $$$ and $$$$ restaurants, even when there is no formal dress code.

Adams-Morgan/Woodley Park

African

$ ✕ **Bukom Café.** Sunny African pop music, a palm-frond-and-*kente*-cloth decor, and a spicy West African menu brighten this narrow two-story dining room. Appetizers include moi-moi and *nklakla* (tomato soup with goat). Entrées range from lamb with melon seeds to *kumasi* (chicken in a peanut sauce) to vegetarian dishes such as *jollof* rice and fried plantains. Live music nightly and late hours (until 2 AM Wednesday, Thursday, and Sunday; until 3 AM Friday–Saturday) keep this place hopping, even by Adams-Morgan standards. ✉ *2442 18th St. NW,* ☎ *202/265–4600. AE, D, MC, V. Closed Mon. No lunch Sun.*

Ethiopian

$-$$ ✕ **Meskerem.** The cuisine of the East African country of
★ Ethiopia abounds in Adams-Morgan, but Meskerem is distinctive for its bright, appealingly decorated dining room and the balcony where you can eat Ethiopian-style—seated on the floor on leather cushions, with large woven baskets for tables. Entrées are served on a large piece of *injera*, a sourdough flatbread; diners eat family style by scooping up mouthful-size portions of the hearty dishes with extra bread. Among Meskerem's specialties are delicious stews made with spicy *berbere* chili sauce, *kitfo*, a buttery beef dish served raw like steak tartare or very rare; and a tangy, green chili vinaigrette potato salad. Combination platters with several different meat or vegetable entrées are avail-

Washington Dining

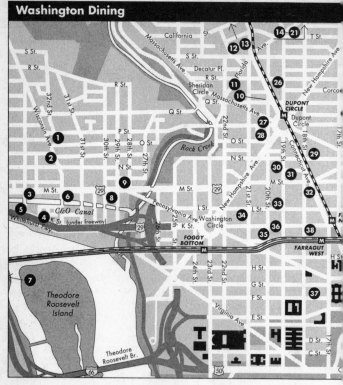

Aditi, **3**

Ben's Chili
Bowl, **24**

Bistro
Français, **6**

Bombay
Club, **39**

Bukom
Café, **15**

Burma, **45**

Café Asia, **33**

Café,
Nema, **23**

Citronelle, **8**

City Lights of
China, **26**

Galileo, **34**

Georgetown
Café, **1**

Georgia
Brown's, **40**

Gerard's
Place, **41**

Hibiscus
Café, **5**

i Ricchi, **30**

Imani Café, **49**

Islander, **14**

La Brasserie, **47**

La
Chaumière, **9**

La Colline, **46**

La
Fourchette, **18**

Le Lion
D'Or, **32**

Maison
Blanche, **37**

a's	Old Ebbitt Grill, **42**	Red Sage, **43**	Skewers-Café Luna, **25**
urant, **16**	Palm, **31**	River Club, **4**	Straits of Malaya, **20**
o's, **22**	Pasta Mia, **17**	Saigon Gourmet, **13**	Tabard Inn, **29**
akesh, **51**	Phillips Flagship, **44**	Sala Thai, **28**	Taberna del Alabardero, **38**
erem, **19**	Pizzeria Paradiso, **27**	Sarinah Satay House, **2**	TomTom, **21**
cle, **50**	Primi Piatti **7, 35**	Sholl's Colonial Cafeteria, **36**	Two Quail, **48**
s, **12**			Vincenzo al Sole, **10**
11			

able as well. ⊠ *2434 18th St. NW,* ☎ *202/462–4100. AE, DC, MC, V.*

French

$$ ✗ **La Fourchette.** On a block in Adams-Morgan where new restaurants are opening almost weekly and closing just as fast, La Fourchette has stayed in business by offering good bistro or French-family-restaurant-style food (chicken in white wine sauce, rich beef stews) at reasonable prices. Most of the menu consists of daily specials and an early-bird fixed-price menu, but you can pretty much count on finding bouillabaisse and rabbit on the list. La Fourchette looks the way a bistro should, with an exposed brick wall, a tin ceiling, bentwood chairs, and quasi-post-Impressionist murals. ⊠ *2429 18th St. NW,* ☎ *202/332–3077. AE, DC, MC, V. No lunch weekends.*

Italian

$ ✗ **Pasta Mia.** Pasta Mia's Southern Italian appetizers and entrées all cost a palatable $7–$9. Large bowls of steaming pasta are served with a generous layer of fresh grated parmesan. Best-sellers include fusilli broccoli with whole cloves of roasted garlic, rich fettuccine verde, and spicy penne arrabiata. *Tiramisù* served in a teacup with espresso-soaked ladyfingers is an elegant way to finish a meal. No wonder area chefs sneak in here on their nights off. ⊠ *1790 Columbia Rd. NW,* ☎ *202/328–9114. MC, V. No lunch.*

Malaysian

$$ ✗ **Straits of Malaya.** Just far enough away from Dupont Circle to be quaint, Straits of Malaya serves some of the most exotic food in Washington—Malaysian/Singaporean cuisine that borrows from Chinese, Thai, and Indian cooking. Dishes—among them chicken satay (on skewers), five spice rolls, fiery *laksa* noodle soup, *udang goreng* (shrimp in a coconut milk sauce), and *poh pia* (shredded jicama stir-fried with vegetables)—are lovely combinations of sweet and pepper-hot spices. Dining on Straits' roof during the warm months is one of the city's finer pleasures. ⊠ *1836 18th St. NW,* ☎ *202/483–1483. AE, D, MC, V. No lunch weekends.*

Mediterranean

$$ ✕ **TomTom.** TomTom's trendy menu features tapas of all
sorts—not just traditional Spanish appetizers but also Ital-
ian and New American variations. The food can be quite
good—green salads come topped with shrimp or grilled
chicken and are fresh and generously portioned—but the
real draw is the atmosphere. On warm nights the rooftop
is packed and area artists set up easels to paint while pa-
trons watch. Hip, artsy crowds wait almost an hour on week-
ends for a table. ⊠ *2335 18th St. NW,* ☎ *202/588–1300.
AE, D, DC, MC, V.*

Middle Eastern

$ ✕ **Mama Ayesha's Restaurant.** Journalists and politicians
(autographed pictures of the last two presidents hang
prominently) are known to frequent Ayesha's for the rea-
sonably priced fare. At the family-run eatery, staples like
chicken and lamb kebobs can be had for less than $10, and
the crisp falafels (spicy vegetable fritters) are some of the
best in town. ⊠ *1967 Calvert St. NW,* ☎ *202/232–5431.
No credit cards.*

New American

$$$ ✕ **New Heights.** With its precise geometrical design soft-
ened by pastel colors, New Heights is one of Washington's
most attractive restaurants specializing in New American
cuisine, in which traditional American and more exotic food
ingredients are combined in innovative ways. Salmon, a frequent offering, might be grilled with vegetables, Swiss
chard, and horseradish beurre blanc. Mustard-grilled quail
in a port wine sauce might be accompanied by wild rice and
croquettes made from quinoa, a high–protein grain from
South America that tastes like couscous. Complimentary
valet parking is an added benefit in an area where parking
can be difficult. ⊠ *2317 Calvert St. NW,* ☎ *202/234–4110.
AE, D, DC, MC, V. No lunch Mon.–Sat.*

Trinidadian

$ ✕ **Islander.** Don't be fooled by appearances—this authen-
★ tic, upstairs Trinidadian roost turns out some of Washington's most exciting and satisfying food. Tangy soup made
with vegetables and marinated fish, delicious *accra* cod frit-
ters, curried goat, and the best and lightest dough-enveloped

rôti you'll ever taste will leave your tastebuds delirious with pleasure. ✉ *1762 Columbia Rd. NW, 2nd floor,* ☎ *202/234–4955. No credit cards. Closed Sun. and Mon.*

Vietnamese

$$ ✕ **Saigon Gourmet.** Service is brisk and friendly at the popular, French-influenced Saigon Gourmet. The upscale neighborhood patrons return for the ultracrisp *cha-gio* (spring rolls), the savory *pho* (beef broth), seafood soups, and the delicately seasoned and richly sauced entrées. Shrimp Saigon mixes prawns and pork in a peppery marinade, and another Saigon dish—grilled pork with rice crepes—is a Vietnamese variation on Chinese *moo shu*. Bananas flambé make for an entertaining dessert as the waiter seems to pour flames from one plate to the other. ✉ *2635 Connecticut Ave. NW,* ☎ *202/265–1360. AE, D, DC, MC, V.*

Capitol Hill

American

$$$ ✕ **Monocle.** The fireplaces and political portraits in a former pair of town houses add to the Monocle's aura of cozy tradition. The restaurant is still probably the best place in Washington for spotting members of Congress at lunch and dinner; its management keeps elected officials informed of when it's time to vote. The cooking—regional American cuisine—is adequate if unexciting and a so-so value, but the old-style Capitol Hill atmosphere, not the food, is the real draw here. Seafood is a specialty; try the crab cakes, and take advantage of the fresh fish specials. ✉ *107 D St. NE,* ☎ *202/546–4488. AE, DC, MC, V. Closed weekends.*

$$ ✕ **Two Quail.** A welcome respite from the men's club atmosphere of traditional Capitol Hill eateries, this quaint, floral-pattern tearoom is tops among women for both romantic and power dining. The seasonal menu has both rich fare—apricot-and-sausage-stuffed pork chop, chicken stuffed with cornbread and pecans, game meats or filet mignon—and lighter, seafood pastas and meal-size salads. Service can be leisurely. ✉ *320 Massachusetts Ave. NE,* ☎ *202/543–8030. AE, D, DC, MC, V. No lunch weekends.*

French

$$$ ✕ **La Brasserie.** One of Capitol Hill's most pleasant and satisfying restaurants, La Brasserie occupies two floors of adjoining town houses, with outdoor dining in season. The basically French menu changes seasonally, with such specials as poached salmon or breast of duck added daily. The crème brûlée, served cold or hot with fruit, is superb. ⊠ *239 Massachusetts Ave. NE,* ☎ *202/546–9154. AE, DC, MC, V.*

$$$ ✕ **La Colline.** Chef Robert Gréault has worked to make La
★ Colline one of the city's best French restaurants—and it is. The menu emphasizes seafood, with offerings ranging from simple grilled preparations to fricassées and gratins with imaginative sauces. Other items usually include duck with orange or cassis sauce and veal with chanterelle mushrooms. ⊠ *400 N. Capitol St. NW,* ☎ *202/737–0400. AE, DC, MC, V. Closed Sun. No lunch Sat.*

Seafood

$$ ✕ **Phillips Flagship.** Cavernous rooms and capacious decks overlook the Capitol Yacht Club's marina. There's a sushi bar (Mon.–Sat.), a party room with its own deck, catering rooms, and space for 1,400. Despite its size, Phillips Flagship serves excellent seafood with dispatch. Succulent softshell crabs, large crab cakes, and blackened catfish are accompanied by chunky fresh vegetables cooked to crunchy perfection. ⊠ *900 Water St. SW,* ☎ *202/488–8515. AE, D, DC, MC, V.*

Southern

$ ✕ **Imani Café.** On the edge of historic Anacostia, one of the Capitol's oldest African-American communities, the Imani Café is already a neighborhood institution. Chicken or fish (baked or fried), spicy black-eyed peas, and peach cobbler are menu regulars. Baked macaroni and cheese and sweet iced-tea punch alone are worth the trip. A great way to end a visit to Frederick Douglass's house or the Smithsonian at Anacostia, with its changing exhibits on African-American culture, the Imani Café lets a family of four eat heartily for less than $30. ⊠ *1918 Martin Luther King Blvd.,* ☎ *202/678–4890. AE, MC, V.*

Downtown

American

$$$$ ✕ **Palm.** Food trends come and go, but the Palm pays no attention; it offers the same hearty food it always has—gargantuan steaks and Nova Scotia lobsters, several kinds of potatoes, and New York cheesecake. Its plain decor is patterned after the New York original, and the businesslike air is matched by the pin-striped clientele. The Palm also offers a bargain lunch menu that includes shrimp, veal, and chicken salad. ⊠ *1225 19th St. NW,* ☎ *202/293–9091. AE, DC, MC, V. No lunch weekends.*

$$ ✕ **Old Ebbitt Grill.** The Old Ebbitt Grill does more business than almost any other eatery in town. People flock here to drink at the several bars, which seem to go on for miles, and to enjoy the oyster bar and carefully prepared bar food that includes buffalo chicken wings, hamburgers, and Reuben sandwiches. But this is not just a place for casual nibbling; the Old Ebbitt offers serious diners homemade pastas and daily specials that emphasize fish dishes and steak. Despite the crowds, the restaurant never feels cramped, thanks to its well-spaced, comfortable booths. Service can be slow at lunch. ⊠ *675 15th St. NW,* ☎ *202/347–4800. AE, DC, MC, V.*

$ ✕ **Sholl's Colonial Cafeteria.** Their slogan is, "Where good foods are prepared right, served right, and priced right"— and truer words were never spoken. Suited federal workers line up next to pensioners and visiting students to grab a bite at this Washington institution, where favorites include chopped steak, liver and onions, and baked chicken and fish. Sholl's is famous for its apple, blueberry, peach, and other fruit pies, but all the desserts are scrumptious and cost around $1. ⊠ *1990 K St. NW,* ☎ *202/296–3065. No credit cards.*

Asian

$ ✕ **Burma.** That Burma the country is bordered by India, ★ Thailand, and China gives some indication of the cuisine at Burma the restaurant, an exquisite jewel in fading Chinatown. Here curry and tamarind share pride of place with lemon, cilantro, and soy seasonings. Batter-fried eggplant and squash are deliciously paired with complex, peppery sauces. Green Tea Leaf and other salads, despite their odd-sounding names and ingredients, leave the tongue with a pleasant tingle. Such entrées as mango pork, tamarind fish, and Kokang chicken are equally satisfying. Bring a group and explore several options on the menu. The very reasonable prices (nothing is over $10) make this easy to do. ⊠ *740 6th St. NW,* ☎ *202/638–1280. AE, D, DC, MC, V. No lunch weekends.*

$ ✕ **Café Asia.** One of Washington's best pan-Asian restaurants, Café Asia presents Japanese, Chinese, Thai, Singaporean, Indonesian, Malayasian, and Vietnamese variations on succulent themes. Highlights include grilled shrimp paste on sugarcane, moist satays, spicy fish in banana leaves, and noodle soups. The dining area covers three floors, the decor is spartan, and the staff is small, but low prices and the chance to try many different types of food in one great place make waits worthwhile. ⊠ *1134 19th St. NW,* ☎ *202/659–2696. AE, DC, MC, V. Closed Sun.*

French

$$$$ ✕ **Le Lion D'Or.** Other French restaurants may flirt with fads,
★ but Le Lion D'Or sticks to the classics—or at any rate the neoclassics—and does them so well that its popularity remains undiminished year after year. If you've ever wondered why so many gourmets rave about French food, Le Lion D'Or's lobster soufflé, crepes with oysters and caviar, and roast pigeon with mushrooms provide delectable answers. The fabulous dessert soufflés may be filled with raspberries or orange essence, or try the sinful chocolate soufflé surrounded by vanilla creme anglaise; all must be ordered in advance. ⊠ *1150 Connecticut Ave. NW (entrance on 18th St. NW),* ☎ *202/296–7972. Jacket and tie. AE, DC, MC, V. Closed Sun. No lunch.*

$$$$ ✕ **Maison Blanche.** A power-broker favorite, Maison Blanche owes its bipartisan popularity not only to its location near the White House and executive office buildings but also to its Old World elegance, the friendliness of the family that runs it, and its large repertoire of classic and modern French dishes, primarily fish. Exceptional are the rich lobster bisque, pastas, and mustard-seasoned rack of lamb. In addition, Maison Blanche goes to great lengths to obtain Dover sole, which it serves grilled or sautéed with butter and lemon. Although Dover sole is usually thought

of as a British dish, Maison Blanche's version is the restaurant's most-ordered entrée. Warm caramel soufflé served with Armagnac liqueur ice cream is a popular dessert. ⊠ *1725 F St. NW,* ☎ *202/842–0070. AE, DC, MC, V. Closed Sun. No lunch Sat.*

Indian

$$–$$$ ✕ **Bombay Club.** One block from the White House, the beau-
  ★   tiful Bombay Club tries to re-create the kind of solace the Beltway elite might have found in a private club had they been 19th-century British colonials in India rather than late-20th-century Washingtonians. The bar, which serves hot hors d'oeuvres at cocktail hour, is furnished with rattan chairs and paneled with dark wood. The dining room, with potted palms and a bright blue ceiling above white plaster moldings, is elegant and decorous. The menu includes unusual seafood specialties and a large number of vegetarian dishes, but the real standouts are the breads and the seafood appetizers. ⊠ *815 Connecticut Ave. NW,* ☎ *202/659–3727. AE, DC, MC, V. No lunch Sat.*

International

$$$ ✕ **Gerard's Place.** With a main dining room strikingly col-
 ★   ored in gray and burnt umber, Gerard's Place concentrates on such fresh, intriguingly prepared entrées as poached lobster with a ginger, lime, and Sauternes sauce; venison served with dried fruits and pumpkin and beetroot purees; and seared tuna with black olives and roasted red peppers. Desserts like the chocolate tear, a teardrop-shaped flourless chocolate cake veined with raspberry, are exquisite. ⊠ *915 15th St. NW,* ☎ *202/737–4445. AE, MC, V. Closed Sun. No lunch Sat.*

Italian

$$$$ ✕ **Galileo.** A spacious, popular restaurant boasting home-
  ★   made everything, from bread sticks to mozzarella, Galileo, in the Adams-Morgan neighborhood, offers risotto, a long list of grilled fish, a game bird dish (such as quail, guinea hen, or woodcock), and at least one or two beef or veal dishes. Preparations are generally simple. For example, the veal chop might be served with mushroom-and-rosemary sauce, the beef with black-olive sauce and polenta. ⊠ *1110 21st St. NW,* ☎ *202/293–7191. AE, D, DC, MC, V. No lunch weekends.*

$$$ ✕ **i Ricchi.** An airy dining room decorated with terra-cotta
★ tiles, cream-colored archways, and floral frescoes, i Ricchi
is priced for expense accounts and remains a favorite of crit-
ics and upscale crowds for its earthy cuisine from the North-
ern Italian province of Tuscany. The spring/summer menu
includes such offerings as rolled pork and rabbit roasted in
wine and fresh herbs, and skewered shrimp; the fall/winter
bill of fare brings grilled lamb chops, thick soups, and
sautéed beef fillet. But whatever the calendar says, I Ricchi
always feels like spring. ✉ *1220 19th St. NW,* ☎ *202/835–
0459. AE, DC, MC, V. Closed Sun. No lunch Sat.*

$$ ✕ **Primi Piatti.** A meal at Primi Piatti—at the D.C. branch,
at least—is like a rush-hour taxi ride in Rome: The crowds
and the noise are overwhelming, but you'll never forget the
trip. Here you get the real thing—not Americanized Italian—
and the food is light and healthful to boot. Several kinds of
fish—tuna with raisins and pine nuts is one preparation—
as well as lamb and veal chops, sizzle each day on a wood-
burning grill. Meats, also cooked on a rotisserie, are succulent;
pastas and pizzas are rewarding, too. ✉ *2013 I St. NW,* ☎
202/223–3600; ✉ *8045 Leesburg Pike, Vienna, VA,* ☎ *703/
893–0300. AE, DC, MC, V. No lunch weekends.*

Moroccan

$$ ✕ **Marrakesh.** A happy surprise is Marrakesh, a bit of
Morocco in a part of the city better known for auto-sup-
ply shops. The menu is a fixed-price ($22) feast shared by
everyone at your table and eaten without silverware (flat-
bread, served with the meal, is used as a scoop). Appetiz-
ers consist of a platter of three salads followed by *b'stella,*
a chicken version of Morocco's traditional pigeon pie. For
the first main course, choose from several chicken prepa-
rations. A beef or lamb dish is served next, followed by veg-
etable couscous, fresh fruit, mint tea, and pastries. Belly
dancers put on a nightly show. Alcoholic drinks can really
drive up the tab. ✉ *617 New York Ave. NW,* ☎ *202/393–
9393. Reservations essential. No credit cards. No lunch.*

Southern

$$–$$$ ✕ **Georgia Brown's.** The airy, curving dining room has white
honeycomb windows and an unusual ceiling ornamenta-
tion of bronze ribbons. An elegant "New South" eatery,
Georgia Brown's serves shrimp Carolina-style (with the head

on and steaming grits on the side), grilled salmon and smoked-bacon green beans, and a thick rich she-crab soup. Fried green tomatoes are given the gourmet treatment.⊠ *950 15th St. NW,* ☎ *202/393–4499. AE, DC, MC, V. No lunch Sat.*

Southwestern/Tex-Mex

$$$ ✕ **Red Sage.** Near the White House is an upscale rancher's
★ delight, roping in the likes of George Bush and Bill Clinton for the tony chow. The multimillion-dollar decor has a barbed-wire-and-lizard theme and a pseudo-adobe warren of dining rooms. Upstairs is the chili bar and café, where thrifty trendsetters can enjoy the comparatively inexpensive sandwiches and appetizers. Downstairs, owner Mark Miller's Berkeley-Santa Fe background surfaces in elaborate, artful presentations such as grilled duck breast with *habanero* pepper and fig sausage, spicy lamb chops with wild-mushroom tamale, and red chili risotto—chilis, in fact, are everywhere. The limited selection of entrées includes lighter options as well. ⊠ *605 14th St. NW,* ☎ *202/ 638–4444. AE, D, DC, MC, V. No lunch Sun.*

Spanish

$$$ ✕ **Taberna del Alabardero.** The Spanish spoken in Taberna del Alabardero is a regal Castilian that matches the formal dining room and high-class service. Start with such appetizer-like tapas as fried calamari, proceed to a hefty bowl of gazpacho soup, and venture on to authentic paella, seafood casseroles, and elegant Spanish country dishes. The plush Old World decor and handsome bar create a romantic atmosphere. The clientele is similarly well-heeled and cosmopolitan. ⊠ *1776 I St. NW (entrance on 18th St.),* ☎ *202/429–2200. AE, D, DC, MC, V. Closed Sun. No lunch Sat.*

Dupont Circle

Chinese

$$ ✕ **City Lights of China.** The Art Deco City Lights of China
★ consistently makes the top restaurant critics' lists every year. The traditional Chinese fare is excellent. Less common specialties are deftly cooked as well, among them lamb in a tangy peppery sauce and shark's fin soup. The mint green booths and elegant silk flower arrangements con-

In case you want to see the world.

At American Express, we're here to make your journey a smooth one. So we have over 1,700 travel service locations in over 120 countries ready to help. What else would you expect from the world's largest travel agency?

do more ®

http://www.americanexpress.com/travel

AMERICAN EXPRESS

Travel

And just in case.

We're here with American Express® Travelers Cheques and Cheques *for Two.*® They're the safest way to carry money on your vacation and the surest way to get a refund, practically anywhere, anytime.

Another way we help you...

do more

AMERICAN
EXPRESS

Travelers Cheques

jure up breezy spring days, even in the midst of a frenzied dinner rush. The delicious jumbo shrimp with spicy salt is baked in its shell before being quickly stir-fried with ginger and spices. Seafood items tend to be especially pricy, but there are plenty of reasonably priced options on this extensive menu. ⊠ *1731 Connecticut Ave., NW,* ☎ *202/265-6688. AE, D, DC, MC, V.*

Italian

$$$ ✕ **Vincenzo al Sole.** Here's something rather rare: a restau-
★   rant that has lowered its prices while continuing to offer many of the same dishes with no change in quality. The emphasis is on simply prepared seafood dishes such as *merluzzo alla calabrese* (roasted cod with capers and olives) and *branzino al salmoriglio* (grilled rockfish with oregano). The menu also includes meat and game dishes such as roast duck with polenta. Part of the dining room is in an airy, glass-roof courtyard. ⊠ *1606 20th St. NW,* ☎ *202/667-0047. AE, DC, MC, V. Closed Sun. No lunch Sat.*

$ ✕ **Pizzeria Paradiso.** Sharing a kitchen with the elite Italian restaurant Obelisk, the petite Pizzeria Paradiso sticks to crowd-pleasing basics: pizzas, *panini* (sandwiches stuffed with Italian cured ham, sun-dried tomatoes and basil, or other ingredients) salads, and desserts. The sandwiches are assembled with homemade focaccia. The trompe l'oeil ceiling adds space and light to a simple interior. ⊠ *2029 P St. NW,* ☎ *202/223–1245. DC, MC, V.*

Middle Eastern

$ ✕ **Skewers/Café Luna.** As the name implies, the focus at Skewers is on kebabs, here served with almond-flaked rice or pasta. Lamb with eggplant and chicken with roasted pepper are the most popular variations, but vegetable kebabs and skewers of filet mignon and shrimp are equally tasty. With nearly 20 choices, the appetizer selection is huge. If the restaurant is too crowded, you can enjoy the cheap California eats (shrimp and avocado salad, mozzarella and tomato sandwiches, vegetable lasagna) downstairs at Café Luna (☎ 202/387–4005) or the reading room-coffeehouse upstairs at Luna Books (☎ 202/332–2543). ⊠ *1633 P St. NW,* ☎ *202/387–7400. AE, DC, MC, V.*

New American

$$$ ✕ **Nora.** Although it bills itself as an "organic restaurant," Nora is no collective-run juice bar. The food is sophisticated and attractive, like the quilt-decorated dining room. A good starter might be grilled marinated squid with orange cherry tomatoes and black olives. Entrées—roast monkfish with artichoke broth or rack of lamb with roast peppers, asparagus, and Swiss chard to name some past favorites— exemplify the chef's emphasis on well-balanced, complex ingredients. ⊠ *2213 M St. NW,* ☎ *202/797–4860;* ⊠ *2132 Florida Ave. NW,* ☎ *202/462–5143. MC, V. Closed Sun. No lunch.*

$$$ ✕ **Tabard Inn.** Named after the resting house in Chaucer's *Canterbury Tales,* the Tabard Inn has an old European feel: fading portraits, a mahogany-paneled main lounge, doilies, an upright piano. Similarly, the Tabard's New American cuisine mixes French, American, and other culinary styles. The strongest dishes are slightly dressed up classics like the grilled New York strip steak and sautéed soft shell crabs over wilted greens. For dessert warm strawberry-rhubarb crisp or white-chocolate cheesecake end dinner on a pleasing note. ⊠ *1739 N St. NW,* ☎ *202/833–2668. MC, V.*

Thai

$–$$ ✕ **Sala Thai.** Who says Thai food has to be scalp-sweating hot? Sala Thai will make the food as spicy as you wish, but the chef is interested in flavor, not fire. Among the subtly seasoned offerings are *panang goong* (shrimp in curry-peanut sauce), chicken sautéed with ginger and pineapple, and flounder with a choice of four sauces. Mirrored walls and soft lights soften the ambience of this small downstairs dining room. ⊠ *2016 P St. NW,* ☎ *202/872–1144. AE, DC, MC, V.*

Georgetown/West End

American

$ ✕ **Georgetown Café.** With its unpretentious decor, cheap prices, and eclectic, lowbrow menu, the Georgetown Café is a bit of a neighborhood oddball. Students and blue-collar types are known to frequent the café for its offering of pizzas, gyros, and home-style American favorites like baked chicken and mashed potatoes. As one of D.C.'s few 24-hour operations, the Georgetown Café is also good for a late-night snack. ⊠ *1523 Wisconsin Ave.* ☎ *202/333–0215. D, MC, V.*

Caribbean

$$ ✕ **Hibiscus Café.** African masks and multicolored neon ac-
★ cents hang from the ceiling of the modish restaurant, where weekend crowds are drawn by spicy jerk chicken and flavorful soups (try the butternut-ginger bisque). Perfectly fried calamari and a generous piece of shark in a pocket of fried bread are paired with ginger sauce or tangy pineapple chutney to make delectable starters. The passion fruit punch is potent. Outdoor seating is available. ⊠ *3401 K St. NW,* ☎ *202/965–7170. AE, D, MC, V. No lunch Sat., no dinner Sun. or Mon.*

French

$$$ ✕ **La Chaumière.** A favorite of Washingtonians seeking an escape from the hurly-burly of Georgetown, La Chaumière has the rustic charm of a French country inn, particularly during the winter, when its central stone fireplace warms the room. Fish stew, mussels, and scallops are on the regular menu, and there is usually a grilled fish special. The restaurant also has a devoted following for its meat dishes, which include such hard-to-find entrées as venison. Many local diners plan their meals around La Chaumière's rotating specials, particularly the couscous on Wednesday and the tasty boiled stew known as cassoulet on Thursday. ⊠ *2813 M St. NW,* ☎ *202/338–1784. Reservations essential. AE, DC, MC, V. Closed Sun. No lunch Sat.*

$$ ✕ **Bistro Français.** Washington's chefs head for Bistro Français for the minute steak maître d'hôtel or the sirloin with herb butter. Among amateur eaters the big draw is the rotisserie chicken. Daily specials may include *suprême* of salmon with broccoli mousse and beurre blanc. The restaurant is divided into two parts—the café side and the more formal dining room; the café menu includes sandwiches and omelets in addition to entrées. The Bistro also offers $11.95 fixed-price lunches and $16.95 early and late-night dinner specials. It stays open until 3 AM Sunday–Thursday, 4 AM

Friday and Saturday. ⊠ *3128 M St. NW,* ☎ *202/338–3830. AE, DC, MC, V.*

Indian

$$ ✕ **Aditi.** Aditi's two-story dining room—with its burgundy carpets and chairs and pale, mint-colored walls with brass sconces—seems too elegant for a moderately priced Indian restaurant. Tandoori and curry dishes are expertly prepared and, for those who like their Indian food on the mild side, not aggressively spiced; if you want your food spicy request it. Rice *biryani* entrées are good for lighter appetites. ⊠ *3299 M St. NW,* ☎ *202/625–6825. AE, DC, MC, V.*

Indonesian

$$ ✕ **Sarinah Satay House.** A green door opens onto stairs that ★ lead down, then up and out into a lush, enclosed garden with real trees growing through the ceiling. The food here is exquisite. Potato croquettes and the traditional *loempia* and *resoles* (crisp and soft spring rolls) come with a tangy, chili-spiked peanut dipping sauce, while the perfectly grilled chicken satay is accompanied by a smoky-sweet peanut dip. At under $10, the combination *nasi rames*—chicken in coconut sauce, beef skewers, and spicy green beans with rice—is a bargain. ⊠ *1338 Wisconsin Ave. NW,* ☎ *202/ 337–2955. AE, D, DC, MC, V. Closed Mon. No lunch Sun.*

New American

$$$ ✕ **Citronelle.** The essence of California chic, Citronelle's ★ glass-front kitchen allows diners to see all the action as chefs scurry to and fro, creating culinary masterpieces. Loin of venison is served with an endive tart and garnished with dried apples. Leek-encrusted salmon steak is topped by a crisp fried-potato lattice. Desserts are equally luscious. The crunchy napoleon—layers of carmelized filo dough between creamy vanilla custard—is drizzled with butterscotch and dark chocolate. A special chef's table gives lucky diners an inside view for a fixed price of $85. ⊠ *3000 M St. NW,* ☎ *202/625–2150. AE, DC, MC, V.*

$$$ ✕ **River Club.** Until someone invents a time machine, there is no better way to experience the Big Band era than to take a trip to the River Club, an Art Deco extravaganza in an out-of-the-way part of Georgetown. Decorated in ebony, silver, neon, and marble, the River Club is in fact a nightclub with a disc jockey who plays everything from '30s and '40s music to contemporary dance music; there's live music Wednesday, Thursday, and Saturday. Start your meal with Chinese smoked lobster; finish with layered white and dark chocolate mousse. Or stick with caviar and champagne. ⊠ *3223 K St. NW,* ☎ *202/333–8118. Jacket and tie. AE, DC, MC, V. Closed Mon. and Tues. No lunch.*

U Street

American

$ ✕ **Ben's Chili Bowl.** Long before U Street became a center of hipness, Ben's was offering patrons chili on hot dogs, chili on smoked sausages, chili on burgers, and chili just about any other way people like it. With its long faux-marble bar and shiny red-vinyl stools, it doesn't look like it has changed much. One concession to modern times is that Ben's offers turkey and vegetarian burgers. Add some cheese fries for a dollar more and you'll be in cholesterol heaven. Ben's is usually open until 2 or 3 AM. ⊠ *1213 U St. NW,* ☎ *202/667–0909. No credit cards.*

Caribbean

$–$$ ✕ **Mango's.** Wood tables washed in bold primary colors, high ceilings, artsy metalwork, and wall-size paintings enhance the pulsing energy of Mango's, an ultra-hip addition to U Street. The Caribbean-influenced fare is a fusion of many different ethnic cooking styles. Smoky Caesar salad comes with plantain chips instead of croutons; coconut curried shrimp is paired with gingered vegetables. ⊠ *2017 14th St. NW,* ☎ *202/332–2104. AE, MC, V. Closed Mon.*

International

$ ✕ **Café Nema.** The Café Nema's eclectic menu combines Somali, North African, and Middle Eastern cuisines. Entrées are simple but flavorful. Grilled chicken, lamb and beef kabobs, and salmon steak are paired with fresh vegetables and an outstanding curried Basmati rice pilaf that has bits of carmelized onion, whole cloves and raisins mixed in. At $3, the generous, made-to-order falafel sandwich may well be the best bargain in the city. ⊠ *1334 U St. NW,* ☎ *202/667–3215. AE, D, DC, MC, V.*

4 Lodging

VISITORS WHO PLAN to spend the night, a week, or a month in D.C. will find a large variety of accommodations from which to choose. Hostelries include grand hotels with glorious histories, quiet Victorian inns, the hotel and motel chains common to every American city, and small independently operated hotels that offer little more than a good location, and a clean place to lay your head.

By Jan Ziegler

Updated by Nancy Ryder

Because Washington is an international city, nearly all hotel staffs are multilingual. All hotels in the $$$ and $$$$ categories have concierges; some in the $$ group do, too. All the hotels we list are air-conditioned. All the large hotels and many of the smaller ones offer meeting facilities and special teleconferencing features for business travelers, ranging from state-of-the-art equipment to modest conference rooms with outside catering. Nearly all the finer hotels have superb restaurants whose traditionally high prices are almost completely justified. Reservations are always crucial.

The hotel reviews here are grouped within neighborhoods according to price. Hotels' parking fees range from $5 to $15 a night, depending on how close to downtown you are.

CATEGORY	COST*
$$$$	over $190
$$$	$145–$190
$$	$100–$145
$	under $100

All prices are for a standard double room, excluding room tax (13% in DC, 12% in MD, and 9.75% in VA) and $1.50 per night occupancy tax.

Capitol Hill

$$$ ☎ **Phoenix Park Hotel.** Named after an historic park in Dublin, the Phoenix Park calls itself "the center of Irish hospitality in America." Near Union Station and only four blocks from the Capitol, the posh high-rise hostelry has an Irish club theme and is home to the Dubliner, one of Washington's best bars. In warm weather it's open for alfresco dining; Irish entertainers perform nightly. The Powerscourt

Restaurant, named after an Irish castle, is a favorite among Washington powerbrokers for its popular Celtic-Continental fare. A $23 million renovation in progress will add more than 70 new guest rooms and health club. ⊠ *520 N. Capitol St. NW, 20001,* ☎ *202/638–6900 or 800/824–5419,* FAX *202/393–3236. 87 rooms, 3 penthouse suites. 2 restaurants, access to health club, laundry service, parking (fee). AE, DC, MC, V.*

$$ 🏨 **Bellevue Hotel.** The charming Bellevue Hotel has been in business since 1929, the year of the stock market crash. Its public rooms on the main floor have balconies and are modeled after great halls in manor houses of yore. Accommodations here are standard modest-hotel fare—some in need of refurbishment—but the staff is friendly. The location is convenient, near Union Station and major Metro stations and within six blocks of the Supreme Court and the Smithsonian museums. ⊠ *15 E St. NW, 20001,* ☎ *202/638–0900 or 800/327–6667,* FAX *202/638–5132. 138 rooms, 2 suites. Restaurant, bar, room service, library, free parking. AE, DC, MC, V.*

$ 🏨 **Holiday Inn Capitol Hill.** For clean, comfortable, low-priced rooms with high-priced views, this is the place. A good value for budget-minded travelers (some rooms are $79), the Holiday Inn Capitol Hill offers the same magnificent views of the Capitol building as the pricier Hyatt, plus a convenient location. Children under age 18 stay free. ⊠ *415 New Jersey Ave. NW, 20001,* ☎ *202/638–1616 or 800/638–1116,* FAX *202/347–1813. 341 rooms, 5 suites. Restaurant, bar, room service, pool, parking (fee). AE, DC, MC, V.*

Downtown

$$$$ 🏨 **Capital Hilton.** There are three reasons to stay at the Capital Hilton: location, location, and location. The place is always jumping because it's near the White House and many monuments; it's also in the middle of the K Street business corridor. The Twigs restaurant has better food and service than the on-site Trader Vic's; still, the ticky-tacky tropical theme of the latter is a tradition with some businesspeople and beloved by many leisure travelers as well. ⊠ *1001 16th St. NW, 20036,* ☎ *202/393–1000 or 800/445–*

8667, FAX *202/639–5726. 515 rooms, 36 suites. 2 restaurants, room service, beauty salon, health club, laundry service and dry cleaning, parking (fee). AE, DC, MC, V.*

$$$$ 🏨 **Carlton Hotel.** Entering the Carlton is like stepping into an updated Italian Renaissance mansion. In the opulent lobby—with its gilded ornamental ceiling and Louis XVI furnishings—you might run into Queen Elizabeth II or the chairman of the World Bank; the hotel has long been a favorite of leaders in business, politics, and society. In a bustling business sector near the White House, the Carlton offers cordial, dignified service. The ornate Allegro dining room—with hand-carved mahogany bar, Italian marble floor, and large Palladian windows—serves Continental cuisine; its buffet lunch and Sunday brunch get rave reviews. An exercise room is equipped with the latest gear. A Carlton Kids program offers savings and goodies; ask for details. ✉ *923 16th St. NW, 20006,* ☎ *202/638–2626 or 800/325–3535,* FAX *202/638–4231. 183 rooms, 14 suites. Restaurant, bar, room service, exercise room, parking (fee). AE, DC, MC, V.*

$$$$
★ 🏨 **Hay-Adams Hotel.** An Italian Renaissance landmark a stone's throw from the White House—rooms on the south side have a view to die for, worth making a reservation for well in advance to enjoy—the Hay-Adams has an eclectic grandeur inside: European and Oriental antiques; Doric, Ionic, and Corinthian touches; carved walnut wainscotting; and intricate ornamental ceilings. It sits on the site of houses owned by statesman and author John Hay and diplomat and historian Henry Adams. The hotel's afternoon tea is renowned. ✉ *1 Lafayette Sq. NW, 20006,* ☎ *202/638–6600 or 800/424–5054,* FAX *202/638–2716. 125 rooms, 18 suites. 2 restaurants, bar, room service, laundry service and dry cleaning, parking (fee). AE, DC, MC, V.*

$$$$
★ 🏨 **Jefferson Hotel.** Next door to the National Geographic Society and opposite the Russian Embassy, the Jefferson's undistinguished beaux-arts exterior is deceiving; inside this small luxury hotel, Federal-style finery abounds. The 100 rooms and suites are each unique in decor and furnished with antiques, original art, VCRs, and CD players; choose selections from the hotel's library or pack your own. The restaurant is a favorite of high-ranking politicos and film stars. A high staff-to-guest ratio ensures outstanding ser-

Washington Lodging

Bellevue
Hotel, **26**

Capital
Hilton, **17**

Carlton
Hotel, **19**

Four Seasons
Hotel, **3**

Georgetown
Suites, **2**

Hay-Adams
Hotel, **20**

Henley Park
Hotel, **22**

Holiday Inn
Capitol Hill, **27**

Hotel Sofitel
Washington, **9**

Hotel Tabard
Inn, **14**

Hotel
Washington, **23**

Jefferson
Hotel, **16**

Kalorama Guest
House, **13**

Latham
Hotel, **1**

Madison
Hotel, **18**

Morrison-
Clark Inn
Hotel, **21**

Normandy
Inn, **11**

Omni
Shoreham
Hotel, **12**

Park Hyatt, **6**

Phoenix Park
Hotel, **25**

Ritz-Carlton, **7**

River Inn, **4**

Stouffer
Renaissance
Mayflower, **15**

Washington
Courtyard by
Marriott, **8**

Washington
Hilton and
Towers, **10**

Watergate
Hotel, **5**

Willard Inter-
Continental, **24**

vice. Employees greet you by name; laundry is hand ironed and delivered in wicker baskets. ⊠ *1200 16th St. NW, 20036,* ☎ *202/347–2200 or 800/368–5966,* FAX *202/785–1505. 68 rooms, 32 suites. Restaurant, bar, room service, in-room VCRs, access to health club, laundry service, concierge, parking (fee). AE, DC, MC, V.*

$$$$ 🏨 **Madison Hotel.** Old World luxury and meticulous service prevail in the Madison (named for fourth U.S. president), which is why the signatures of presidents, prime ministers, sultans, and kings fill the guest register, as well as those of just plain well-to-do folks who appreciate punctilious European standards. Deceivingly contemporary on the outside, the 14-story building, four blocks from the White House, owns a world-class collection of antiques—a rare Chinese Imperial altar table and a Louis XVI palace commode are on display in the lobby. The Montpelier restaurant, specializing in Continental cuisine, is art-filled and posh. ⊠ *15th and M Sts. NW, 20005,* ☎ *202/862–1600 or 800/424–8577,* FAX *202/785–1255. 318 rooms, 35 suites. 2 restaurants, bar, room service, exercise room, parking (fee). AE, DC, MC, V.*

$$$$ 🏨 **Stouffer Renaissance Mayflower.** Franklin Delano Roosevelt wrote "We have nothing to fear but fear itself" in Suite 776. J. Edgar Hoover dined here at the same table every day for 20 years. Ever since the 10-story Stouffer Renaissance Mayflower opened in 1925 for Calvin Coolidge's inauguration it has been making history makers (and leisure travelers) feel at home, and this national historic landmark, four blocks from the White House, continues to be a central part of Washington life. Sunlight spills into the majestic skylit lobby, causing the gilded trim to gleam; Oriental rugs splash the floors with color; sculpted cherubs prance around trees that brachiate into electrified candelabra. Contemporary seafood is served amid silver, crystal, and artful flower arrangements at the Nicholas restaurant. ⊠ *1127 Connecticut Ave. NW, 20036,* ☎ *202/347–3000 or 800/468–3571,* FAX *202/466–9082. 660 rooms, 81 suites. 2 restaurants, bar, room service, sauna, exercise room, shops, parking (fee). AE, DC, MC, V.*

$$$$ 🏨 **Willard Inter-Continental.** "I am surely glad to be under
★   your roof," declared Abraham Lincoln when entering the Willard Hotel on arrival in Washington as the nation's

16th president. Indeed, the Willard, whose present building dates from 1901, welcomed every American president from Franklin Pierce in 1853 to Dwight Eisenhower in the 1950s before closing after years of decline. The new Willard, a faithful renovation, is an opulent beaux arts feast to the eye, as the main lobby, with its spectacular proportions, great columns, huge chandeliers, mosaic floors, and elaborately carved ceilings attests. The hotel's formal eatery, the Willard Room, has won nationwide acclaim for its use of classic French and modern cuisine nouvelle techniques to enliven dishes from France, Germany, and the U.S. South. ⊠ *1401 Pennsylvania Ave. NW, 20004,* ☎ *202/628–9100 or 800/327–0200,* 𝖥𝖠𝖷 *202/637–7326. 341 rooms, 38 suites. 2 restaurants, 2 bars, minibars, room service, health club, laundry service and dry cleaning, shops, meeting rooms, parking (fee). AE, DC, MC, V.*

$$$ 🏨 **Henley Park Hotel.** A Tudor-style building adorned with
★ 119 gargoyles, this National Historic Trust hotel with the charm of an English country house is unique in downtown Washington. The main eatery, Coeur de Lion, has a leafy atrium, stained glass windows, a pleasant English air, and a decidedly un-English menu in which such dishes as goat cheese-and-bell pepper ravioli and poached salmon with buckwheat noodles have Mediterranean and Asian accents. A bit far from the attractions of the Mall to walk and in a less-than-great neighborhood (take a cab after dark), Henley Park is nevertheless only a short ride on public transportation from the major sights; limousine service, gracious Old World atmosphere, and an attentive staff make it worth considering, especially if you like bed-and-breakfasts and country inns. ⊠ *926 Massachusetts Ave. NW, 20001,* ☎ *202/638–5200 or 800/222–8474,* 𝖥𝖠𝖷 *202/638–6740. 79 rooms, 17 suites. Restaurant, bar, room service, access to health club, parking (fee). AE, DC, MC, V.*

$$ 🏨 **Hotel Washington.** Since opening in 1918 the Hotel
★ Washington has been known for its view. Washingtonians bring visitors to the outdoor rooftop bar for cocktails and a panorama that includes the White House grounds and Washington Monument. The oldest continuously operating hostelry in the city and now a national landmark, it sprang from the drawing boards of John Carrère and Thomas Hastings, who designed the New York Public Library. Some

rooms look directly onto the White House lawn. Suite 506 is where Elvis Presley stayed on his trips to D.C. ⊠ *515 15th St. NW, 20004,* ☎ *202/638–5900,* FAX *202/638–1594. 344 rooms, 16 suites. Restaurant, bar, deli, lobby lounge, room service, exercise room, laundry service and dry cleaning, business services. AE, DC, MC, V.*

$$ 🏨 **Morrison-Clark Inn Hotel.** A merger of two 1864 town
★   houses, the airy Victorian Morrison-Clark Hotel is a National Trust for Historic Preservation-designated Historic Hotel. One house has a 1917 Chinese Chippendale porch; Oriental touches echo throughout the public rooms, which include marble fireplaces and 14-foot-high mirrors with original gilding. Antique-filled rooms—some with bay windows, fireplaces, or access to a porch—have different personalities; one is called the "deer and bunny room" because of its decorative trim. The restaurant's New American–Southern cuisine has been roundly praised. ⊠ *Massachusetts Ave. and 11th St. NW, 20001,* ☎ *202/898–1200 or 800/332–7898,* FAX *202/289–8576. 54 rooms. CP. Restaurant, room service, exercise room, laundry service and dry cleaning, parking (fee). AE, D, DC, MC, V.*

Dupont Circle

$$$$ 🏨 **Ritz-Carlton.** The childhood home of Al Gore, the intimate Ritz-Carlton has an English hunt-club theme; rooms have views of Embassy Row or Georgetown and the National Cathedral. The pricey Jockey Club restaurant, with its half-timber ceilings, dark wood paneling, and red-checker tablecloths, draws the crowned heads of Washington. The Fairfax Bar is a cozy spot for a drink beside the fire (with piano entertainment some evenings). Guests have access to a nearby golf course, pool, and tennis courts. ⊠ *2100 Massachusetts Ave. NW, 20008,* ☎ *202/293–2100 or 800/241–3333,* FAX *202/466–9867. 174 rooms, 32 suites. Restaurant, bar, minibars, room service, in-room VCRs, massage, sauna, exercise room, meeting rooms. AE, DC, MC, V.*

$$$ 🏨 **Hotel Sofitel Washington.** With the ambience of a European luxury hostelry, the Hotel Sofitel Washington may be
★   small, but its rooms are among the largest in any Washington hotel. The Trocadero Café serves three meals daily. ⊠ *1914 Connecticut Ave. NW, 20009,* ☎ *202/797–2000 or*

800/424–2464, FAX *202/462–0944. 108 rooms, 37 suites. Restaurant, bar, room service, access to health club, laundry service and dry cleaning, parking (fee). AE, DC, MC, V.*

$$$ ⊞ **Washington Hilton and Towers.** A busy convention hotel,
★ the Washington Hilton is as much an event as a place to stay. You might run into a leading actor, cabinet official, or six busloads of towheaded teenagers from Utah in the lobby. Guest rooms are compact but light-filled, and the hotel is convenient, a short walk from the shops and restaurants of Dupont Circle and the Adams-Morgan neighborhood. ⊠ *1919 Connecticut Ave. NW, 20009,* ☏ *202/ 483–3000 or 800/445–8667,* FAX *202/265–8221. 1,062 rooms, 88 suites. 3 restaurants (1 seasonal), 2 bars, room service, pool, 3 tennis courts, health club, shops, parking (fee). AE, DC, MC, V.*

$$ ⊞ **Washington Courtyard by Marriott.** One of the city's best
★ values for budget travelers, Marriott's Washington Courtyard hotel is a good alternative for international tourists and businesspeople who can't find rooms at the Washington Hilton. Guest rooms on the west and south have good views. Coffee and cookies are served daily in the European-style lobby. ⊠ *1900 Connecticut Ave. NW, 20009,* ☏ *202/ 332–9300 or 800/842–4211,* FAX *202/328–7039. 147 rooms. Restaurant, bar, pool, access to health club, parking (fee). AE, DC, MC, V.*

$ ⊞ **Hotel Tabard Inn.** Formed by a linkage of three Victorian town houses, the Hotel Tabard Inn is one of the oldest continuously running hostelries in D.C. Named after the inn in Chaucer's *Canterbury Tales*, it's furnished throughout with broken-in Victorian and American Empire antiques. Dim lighting and a genteel shabbiness strike some as off-putting, others as charming. Rooms have no TV, there's no room service, and what service there is can be uneven, but the quiet street, the quick walk to Dupont Circle and the K Street business district, and moderate prices for most rooms with private bath make early reservations advisable. ⊠ *1739 N St. NW, 20036,* ☏ *202/785–1277,* FAX *202/785– 6173. 40 rooms, 25 with bath. Restaurant. MC, V.*

Georgetown

$$$$ 🏨 **Four Seasons Hotel.** The Four Seasons Hotel may be a
★   modern brick-and-glass edifice amid Georgetown's 19th century Federal and Georgian row houses, but inside Old
World elegance prevails; the rich mahogany paneling, antiques, spectacular flower arrangements, and impeccable service are hallmarks of a mecca for Washington's elite. Guest
rooms offer a choice of views: of the old C&O Canal, the
trees and streams of Rock Creek Park, the busy Georgetown street scene, or the quiet courtyard. The private night-
club Desirée is open to guests, as is what may be the poshest
hotel health club in America (each Lifecycle machine has
its own Walkman, TV, and VCR). The Four Seasons is
kid-friendly, too, with children's menus, games, and activities, "Tea Time for Tots," and milk and cookies at bed-
time. ⊠ *2800 Pennsylvania Ave. NW, 20007,* ☎ *202/
342–0444 or 800/332–3442,* 🅵🅰🆇 *202/342–1673. 160
rooms, 36 suites. 2 restaurants, bar, room service, pool,
health club, nightclub, parking (fee). AE, DC, MC, V.*

$$$ 🏨 **Latham Hotel.** A small Colonial-style hotel in a lively neigh-
borhood, the Latham has rooms with a sleek, updated look
that contrast with the redbrick, neocolonial exterior. Those
on the M Street side have courtyard views overlooking the
C&O Canal. The hotel is a favorite of Europeans, sports
figures, and devotees of Georgetown. It's Citronelle restau-
rant (☞ Chapter 4) is among the best ⊠ *3000 M St. NW,
20007,* ☎ *202/726–5000 or 800/368–5922,* 🅵🅰🆇 *202/337–
4250. 143 rooms, 9 suites. Restaurant, bar, room service,
pool, access to health club, parking (fee). AE, DC, MC, V.*

$$ 🏨 **Georgetown Suites.** If you consider standard hotel rooms
cramped and overpriced, the all-suite Georgetown Suites—
in a redbrick courtyard one block south of M Street in the
heart of Georgetown—is a find. Suites vary in size but all
have full kitchens, iron and ironing boards, hair dryers, and
voice mail. Continental breakfast is free, as are local phone
calls and long-distance access. You might have to carry your
own bags and the Metro is a 10-minute walk away, but for
comfort and value it's tops. Children under 12 stay free.
⊠ *1111 30th St. NW, 20007,* ☎ *202/298–7800 or
800/348–7203,* 🅵🅰🆇 *202/333–5792. 138 suites. CP. Kitchens,*

exercise room, laundry service and dry cleaning, parking (fee). AE, DC, MC, V.

Northwest/Upper Connecticut Avenue

$$$$ 🏨 **Omni Shoreham Hotel.** Resembling an old-time resort,
★ the Omni Shoreham offers views of the jogging and bike paths of leafy Rock Creek Park and is close to the Adams-Morgan neighborhood, Dupont Circle, and the National Zoo. In back, a pool overlooks a sweeping lawn and woods beyond. Some of the large, light-filled rooms have fireplaces; half face the park. Comedienne Joan Cushing frequently holds forth in the Marquee Lounge, which has a weekend matinee cabaret for children. ✉ *2500 Calvert St. NW, 20008,* ☎ *202/234–0700 or 800/834–6664,* FAX *202/ 332–1373. 720 rooms, 50 suites. Restaurant, bar, snack bar, room service, pool, 3 tennis courts, basketball, exercise room, horseshoes, shuffleboard, shops, cabaret, parking (fee). AE, DC, MC, V.*

$ 🏨 **Kalorama Guest House.** Five separate turn-of-the-cen-
★ tury town houses—three on a quiet street in the Adams-Morgan neighborhood and two in residential Woodley Park—compose the Kalorama Guest House, with its comfortable atmosphere created by dark-wood walls; hand-me-down antique oak furniture; traditional, slightly worn upholstery; brass or antique wooden bedsteads; and calico curtains. The coffeepot is always on, the staff friendly, and guests have the run of each house, its front parlor, and the areas where complimentary breakfast and afternoon aperitifs are served. Rooms range from large to tiny; none has a phone or a TV. The inn in Adams-Morgan is steps from the liveliest section of the neighborhood. The Woodley Park inn is near the National Zoo. Both are a short walk to the Metro. ✉ *1854 Mintwood Pl. NW, 20009,* ☎ *202/ 667–6369,* FAX *202/319–1262. 2700;* ✉ *Cathedral Ave. NW, 20008,* ☎ *202/328–0860. 50 rooms, 30 with bath, 5 suites. CP. AE, DC, MC, V.*

$ 🏨 **Normandy Inn.** A small European-style hotel on a quiet
★ street in the exclusive embassy area of Connecticut Avenue, the Normandy is near restaurants and some of the most expensive residential real estate in Washington. Rooms are standard, functional, and comfortable; all have refrigera-

tors. Each Tuesday evening a wine-and-cheese reception is held for guests. ✉ *2118 Wyoming Ave. NW, 20008,* ☎ *202/483–1350 or 800/424–3729,* FAX *202/387–8241. 65 rooms, 10 suites. CP. Refrigerators, room service, parking (fee). AE, D, MC, V.*

West End/Foggy Bottom

$$$$ ⊞ **Park Hyatt.** With its neoclassical exterior and multicolored marble lobby adorned with masterpieces by such Washington Color Painter school artists as Kenneth Nolan, Gene Davis, and Paul Reed—plus works by Matisse, Leger, Calder, and Picasso—the Park Hyatt is one of Georgetown's toniest places to stay, with carpeting so thick you almost bounce. Bronzes, chinoiserie, and a fortune teller at tea in the main-floor lounge, which overlooks a lovely landscaped garden, are Old World touches that offset the spareness of the hotel's design. The Park's health club features an indoor pool with skylight, saunas, steam rooms, Jacuzzi, and an exercise room stocked with the latest equipment. The elegant, dramatically sunlit Melrose Restaurant serves contemporary American cuisine with an emphasis on seafood. The Kennedy Center is a 3-minute cab ride away. ✉ *1201 24th St. NW, 20037,* ☎ *202/789–1234 or 800/233–1234,* FAX *202/457–8823. 93 rooms, 131 suites. Restaurant, bar, outdoor café, room service, indoor pool, beauty salon, massage, health club, parking (fee). AE, DC, MC, V.*

$$$$ ⊞ **Watergate Hotel.** If you want to stay in the most important
★ hotel in modern American history, scene of the burglary that resulted in the resignation of President Richard Nixon, here it is. The internationally famous Watergate, its distinctive sawtooth design a landmark along the Potomac, offers guests a taste of traditional English gentility. Guest rooms are large; many have balconies and most have striking river views. Accustomed to serving the world's elite, the hotel also welcomes vacationing families and couples on getaway weekends—as long as price is no object. Next door is the Kennedy Center; Georgetown is a short walk away. Complimentary limousine service to Capitol Hill or downtown is available weekdays. ✉ *2650 Virginia Ave. NW, 20037,* ☎ *202/965–2300 or 800/424–2736,* FAX *202/337–7915.*

90 rooms, 146 suites. 2 restaurants, bar, room service, indoor pool, health club, parking (fee). AE, DC, MC, V.

$$ ⊡ **River Inn.** This small all-suite hotel is steps from Georgetown, George Washington University, and the Kennedy Center. On the premises is the cozy Foggy Bottom Café. The best views are from the fourteen Potomac Suites, each of which has a full walk-in kitchen. The lobby is sleek and contemporary, but the room furnishings are homey and modest. This is a popular spot with parents of George Washington University students. ⊠ *924 25th St. NW, 20037,* ☎ *202/337–7600 or 800/424–2741,* ℻ *202/625–2618. 127 suites. Restaurant, room service, use of pool at One Washington Circle and health club at Watergate. AE, DC, MC, V.*

5 Nightlife and the Arts

THE ARTS

By John F.
Kelly

Updated
by Nancy
Ryder

In the past 20 years, Washington has been transformed into a cultural capital. The Kennedy Center is a world-class venue, home of the National Symphony Orchestra and host to Broadway shows, ballet, modern dance, opera, and more. Washington even has its own "off Broadway": a half dozen or so plucky theaters spread out around the city that offer new twists on both old and new works. Several art galleries present highly regarded chamber music series. The service bands from the area's numerous military bases ensure an endless supply of martial music of the John Philip Sousa variety as well as rousing renditions of more contemporary tunes. Washington was the birthplace of *hardcore,* a socially aware form of punk rock music that has influenced young bands throughout the country. *Go-go*—infectious, rhythmic music mixing elements of rap, rhythm and blues, and funk—has been touted as the next big sound to go national but still seems confined largely to Washington.

Friday's *Washington Post* "Weekend" section is the best guide to events for the weekend and the coming week. The *Post*'s daily "Guide to the Lively Arts" also outlines cultural events in the city. The *Washington Times* "Weekend" section comes out on Thursday. The free weekly *Washington CityPaper* hits the streets on Thursday and covers the entertainment scene well. You might also consult the "City Lights" section in the monthly *Washingtonian* magazine.

Any search for cultured entertainment should start at the **John F. Kennedy Center for the Performing Arts** (☞ Foggy Bottom *in* Chapter 2 for details). On any given night America's national cultural center may be hosting a symphony orchestra, a troupe of dancers, a Broadway musical, and a comedy whodunit. In other words, the "KenCen" has a little of everything. It is actually five stages under one roof: the **Concert Hall,** home park of the National Symphony Orchestra; the 2,200-seat **Opera House,** the setting for ballet, modern dance, grand opera, and large-scale musicals; the **Eisenhower Theater,** usually used for drama; the **Terrace Theater,** a Philip Johnson–designed space that showcases chamber groups and experimental works; and the **Theater Lab,** home to cabaret-style performances (since

1987 the audience-participation hit mystery, **Shear Madness**, has been playing here).

Tickets

Tickets to most events are available by calling or visiting each theater's box office.

Protix takes reservations for events at Wolf Trap and elsewhere in the city. It also has outlets in selected Woodward & Lothrop and Safeway stores. ☎ *703/218–6500.*

TicketMaster takes phone charges for events at most venues around the city. You can purchase TicketMaster tickets in person at all Hecht Company department stores. No refunds or exchanges are allowed. ☎ *202/432–7328 or 800/551–7328.*

TicketPlace sells half-price, day-of-performance tickets for selected shows; a "menu board" lists available performances. Only cash is accepted, and there's a 10% service charge per order. TicketPlace also is a full-price TicketMaster outlet. ✉ *Lisner Auditorium, 730 21st St. NW,* ☎ *202/842–5387.* ☉ *Tues.–Fri. noon–4, Sat. 11–5. Tickets for Sun. and Mon. performances sold on Sat.*

Dance

Dance Place. A studio theater that presented its first performance in 1980, Dance Place hosts a wide assortment of modern and ethnic dance most weekends. ✉ *3225 8th St. NE,* ☎ *202/269–1600.*

Smithsonian Associates Program (☞ Smithsonian Institution, *below*). National and international dance groups often perform at various Smithsonian museums. ☎ *202/357–3030.*

Washington Ballet. In October, February, and May this company presents classical and contemporary ballets from the works of such choreographers as George Balanchine, Marius Petipa, and Choo-San Goh, mainly at the Kennedy Center and the Warner Theatre. Each December the Washington Ballet presents *The Nutcracker.* ☎ *202/362–3606.*

Film

American Film Institute. More than 700 different movies—including contemporary and classic foreign and American films—are shown each year at the American Film Institute's theater in the Kennedy Center. Filmmakers and actors are often present to discuss their work. ⊠ *Kennedy Center, New Hampshire Ave. and Rock Creek Pkwy. NW,* ☎ *202/785–4600.*

Cineplex Odeon Uptown. You don't find many like this old beauty anymore: one huge, multiplex-dwarfing screen, Art Deco flourishes instead of a bland boxy interior, a wonderful balcony, and—in one happy concession to modernity–crystalline Dolby sound. Other first-run movie theaters are clustered near Dupont Circle, in Georgetown, and around upper Wisconsin Avenue. ⊠ *3426 Connecticut Ave. NW,* ☎ *202/966–5400.*

Cineplex Odeon's West End 1–4. Closer to downtown than some other theaters, here's a convenient place to catch one of the latest hit films. ⊠ *23rd and L Sts. NW,* ☎ *202/293–3152.*

Hirshhorn Museum. For avant-garde and experimental film lovers, weekly movies—often first-run documentaries, features, and short films—are shown free. ⊠ *8th and Independence Ave. SW,* ☎ *202/357–2700.*

Key. This four-screen theater specializes in foreign films and presents an annual animation festival. ⊠ *1222 Wisconsin Ave. NW,* ☎ *202/333–5100.*

Mary Pickford Theater. A 64-seat theater, the Mary Pickford shows classic and historically important films for free. ⊠ *Jefferson Bldg. of Library of Congress, 1st St. and Independence Ave. SE,* ☎ *202/707–5677.*

National Geographic Society. Educational films with a scientific, geographic, or anthropological focus are shown here weekly. ⊠ *17th and M Sts. NW,* ☎ *202/857–7588.*

West End 5, 6, 7. If you're in the mood for a movie and in the vicinity of downtown Washington, the West End is one of the more conveniently located multiplexes in the Capitol. ⊠ *23rd and M Sts. NW,* ☎ *202/452–9020.*

Music

Concert Halls

DAR Constitution Hall. Constitution Hall was the home of the National Symphony Orchestra before the Kennedy Center was built. The 3,700-seat hall still hosts visiting performers, from jazz to pop to rap. ⊠ *18th and C Sts. NW,* ☎ *202/638–2661.*

Lisner Auditorium. A 1,500-seat theater on the campus of George Washington University, Lisner Auditorium is the setting for pop, classical, and choral music. ⊠ *21st and H Sts. NW,* ☎ *202/994–6800.*

National Gallery of Art. Free concerts by the National Gallery Orchestra, conducted by George Manos, plus performances by outside recitalists and ensembles, are held in the venerable West Building's West Garden Court on Sunday evenings from October to June. Most performances highlight classical music, though April's American Music Festival often features jazz. Entry is first-come, first-served. ⊠ *6th St. and Constitution Ave. NW,* ☎ *202/842–6941 or 202/842–6698.*

Smithsonian Institution (☞ The Mall *in* Chapter 2). A rich assortment of music—both free and ticketed—is presented by the Smithsonian. American jazz, musical theater, and popular standards are performed in the National Museum of American History's Palm Court. In the third-floor Hall of Musical Instruments, musicians periodically perform on historic instruments from the museum's collection. ☎ *202/357–2700.*

Chamber Music

Corcoran Gallery of Art. Hungary's Takacs String Quartet and the Cleveland Quartet are among the chamber groups that appear in the Corcoran's Musical Evening Series, one Friday each month from October to May, with some summer offerings. Concerts are followed by a reception with the artists. ⊠ *17th St. and New York Ave. NW,* ☎ *202/638–3211.*

Folger Shakespeare Library. The Folger Shakespeare Library's internationally acclaimed resident chamber music ensemble, the Folger Consort, regularly presents a selection of instrumental and vocal pieces from the medieval, Renaissance, and Baroque periods, during a season that runs from October to May. ⊠ *201 E. Capitol St. SE,* ☎ *202/544-7077.*

National Academy of Sciences. Free performances by such groups as the Juilliard String Quartet and the Beaux Arts Trio are given October through May in the academy's acoustically nearly perfect 670-seat auditorium. ⊠ *2101 Constitution Ave. NW,* ☎ *202/334-2436.*

Phillips Collection. Duncan Phillips's mansion is more than an art museum. From September through May the long paneled music room hosts Sunday afternoon recitals. Chamber groups from around the world perform; May is devoted to performing artists from the Washington area. The concerts begin at 5 PM. For decent seats, arrive early. ⊠ *1600 21st St. NW,* ☎ *202/387-2151.*

Choral Music

Choral Arts Society. Founded in 1965, the 180-voice Choral Arts Society choir performs a varied selection of classical pieces at the Kennedy Center from September to April. Three Christmas sing-alongs are scheduled each December. ⊠ *New Hampshire Ave. and Rock Creek Pkwy. NW,* ☎ *202/244-3669.*

Washington National Cathedral. Choral and church groups frequently perform in the impressive settings here. ⊠ *Wisconsin and Massachusetts Aves. NW,* ☎ *202/537-6200.*

Orchestra

National Symphony Orchestra. The season at the Kennedy Center extends from September to June. In summer the NSO performs at Wolf Trap and presents concerts on the West Lawn of the Capitol on Memorial Day and Labor Day weekends and on July 4. One of the cheapest ways to hear—if not necessarily see—the NSO perform in the Kennedy Center Concert Hall is to get a $10 "obstructed view" ticket. ⊠ *New Hampshire Ave. and Rock Creek Pkwy NW,* ☎ *202/416-8100.*

Performance Series

Armed Forces Concert Series. From June to August, service bands from all four branches of the military perform marches, patriotic numbers, and some classical music Monday, Tuesday, Thursday, and Friday evenings, on the East Terrace of the Capitol and several nights a week at the Sylvan Theater (☞ *below*) on the Washington Monument grounds. ☎ *Air Force, 202/767–5658; Army, 703/696–3718; Navy, 202/433–2525; Marines, 202/433–4011.*

Carter Barron Amphitheater. On Saturday and Sunday nights from mid-June to August this lovely, 4,250-seat outdoor theater in Rock Creek Park hosts pop, jazz, gospel, and rhythm and blues artists such as Chick Corea, Nancy Wilson, and Tito Puente. ✉ *16th St. and Colorado Ave. NW,* ☎ *202/426–6837; off-season, 202/426–6893.*

Ft. Dupont Summer Theater. When it comes to music in Washington, even the National Park Service gets in on the act. NPS presents national and international jazz artists at 8:30 on Friday and Saturday evenings from mid-June to August at the outdoor Ft. Dupont Summer Theater. Wynton Marsalis, Betty Carter, and Ramsey Lewis are among the artists who have performed at free concerts in the past. ✉ *Minnesota Ave. and F St. SE,* ☎ *202/426–7723 or 202/619–7222.*

Sylvan Theater. Service bands from the four branches of the military perform alfresco at the Sylvan Theater from mid-June to August, Tuesday, Thursday, Friday, and Sunday nights. ✉ *Washington Monument grounds,* ☎ *202/619–7225 or 202/619–7222.*

Opera

Summer Opera Theater Company. An independent professional troupe, the Summer Opera Theater Company mounts two fully staged productions each summer, one in June and one in July. ✉ *Hartke Theater, Catholic University,* ☎ *202/526–1669.*

Washington Opera. Seven operas—presented in their original languages with English supertitles—are performed each season (November–March) in the Kennedy Center's

Opera House and Eisenhower Theater. ☎ *202/416–7800 or 800/876–7372.*

Theater

Commercial Theaters and Companies

Arena Stage. The city's most respected resident company (established 1950), the Arena was the first theater outside New York to win a Tony award. It presents a wide-ranging season in its three theaters: the theater-in-the-round Arena, the proscenium Kreeger, and the cabaret-style Old Vat Room. ✉ *6th St. and Maine Ave. SW,* ☎ *202/488–3300.*

Ford's Theatre. Looking much as it did when President Lincoln was shot at a performance of *Our American Cousin,* Ford's is host mainly to musicals, many with family appeal. ✉ *511 10th St. NW,* ☎ *202/347–4833.*

National Theatre. Destroyed by fire and rebuilt four times, the National Theatre has operated in the same location since 1835. It presents pre- and post-Broadway shows. ✉ *1321 E St. NW,* ☎ *202/628–6161.*

Shakespeare Theatre. Four plays—three by the Bard, another a classic from his era—are staged each year by the acclaimed Shakespeare Theatre troupe. ✉ *450 7th St. NW,* ☎ *202/393–2700.*

Warner Theatre. One of Washington's grand theaters, the 1924 building received a complete face-lift in 1992. The renovated space now hosts road shows, dance recitals, and the occasional pop music act. ✉ *13th and E Sts. NW,* ☎ *202/783–4000.*

Small Theaters and Companies

Gala Hispanic Theatre. The company produces Spanish classics as well as contemporary and modern Latin American plays in both Spanish and English. ✉ *1625 Park Rd. NW,* ☎ *202/234–7174.*

Source Theatre. The 107-seat Source Theatre presents established plays with a sharp satirical edge and modern interpretations of classics. Each July and August, Source hosts the Washington Theater Festival, a celebration of new plays, many by local playwrights. ⊠ *1835 14th St. NW,* ☎ *202/462–1073.*

Studio Theatre. An eclectic season of classic and offbeat plays is presented in this 200-seat theater, one of the nicest among Washington's small, independent companies. ⊠ *1333 P St. NW,* ☎ *202/332–3300.*

Washington Stage Guild. Founded in 1985 and performing in historic Carroll Hall, Washington Stage Guild performs the classics as well as more contemporary fare. Shaw is a specialty. ⊠ *924 G St. NW,* ☎ *202/529–2084.*

Woolly Mammoth. Unusual, imaginatively produced shows have earned Wooly Mammoth good reviews and favorable comparisons to Chicago's Steppenwolf. ⊠ *1401 Church St. NW,* ☎ *202/393–3939.*

NIGHTLIFE

Even though the after-dark scene has contracted a bit in the last few years, Washington's nightlife still offers an array of watering holes, comedy clubs, discos, and intimate musical venues catering to a wide spectrum of customers, from proper political appointees to blue-collar regulars in from the suburbs. Many nightspots are clustered in a few key areas, simplifying things for the visitor who enjoys bar-hopping. Georgetown, in northwest Washington, leads the pack with an explosion of bars, nightclubs, and restaurants on M Street east and west of Wisconsin Avenue and on Wisconsin Avenue north of M Street. A half-dozen Capitol Hill bars can be found on a stretch of Pennsylvania Avenue between 2nd and 4th streets SE. There is another high-density nightlife area around the intersection of 19th and M streets NW.

Your best bet for evening action is to consult Friday's "Weekend" section in the *Washington Post* and the free weekly *Washington CityPaper*. It's also a good idea to call clubs ahead of time to find out who's on that night and what sort of music will be played.

Acoustic/Folk/Country Clubs

Afterwords. Afterwords could just as easi[ly] [be called] words, shoehorned as it is in the Kramer[books at] Dupont Circle. Folkish acts entertain browsing bohemian bookworms as well as patrons seated at a cozy in-store café. ⊠ *1517 Connecticut Ave. NW,* ☎ *202/387–1462.* ☉ *Mon.–Thurs. 7:30 AM–1 AM, Fri. 7:30 AM–Mon. 1 AM.*

Birchmere. It may be in an unpretentious suburban strip mall, but Birchmere is one of the best places this side of the Blue Ridge Mountains to hear acoustic folk and bluegrass acts. Favorite sons the Seldom Scene are Thursday-night regulars. ⊠ *3901 Mt. Vernon Ave., Alexandria, VA,* ☎ *703/549–5919. MC, V.* ☉ *Sun.–Thurs. 6:30 PM–11 PM, Fri. and Sat. 7 PM–12:30 AM.*

Zed Restaurant. Can cowboy hats and boots peacefully co-exist in a city of Brooks Brothers suits? A visit to Zed proves that they can. Each evening, bands in this suburban Virginia night spot play hits from Nashville and other points south and west. Two-stepping is encouraged. ⊠ *6151 Richmond Hwy., Alexandria, VA,* ☎ *703/768–5558. AE, MC, V.* ☉ *Daily 11 AM–2 AM.*

Bars and Lounges

Brickskeller. A beer lover's mecca, Brickskeller is the place to go when you want something more exotic than a Bud Lite. More than 500 brands of beer are for sale—from Central American lagers to U.S. microbrewed ales. Bartenders oblige beer-can collectors by opening the containers from the bottom. ⊠ *1523 22nd St. NW,* ☎ *202/293–1885.* ☉ *Mon.–Thurs. 11:30 AM–2 AM, Fri. 11:30 AM–3 AM, Sat. 6 PM–3 AM, Sun. 6 PM–2 AM.*

Capitol City Brewing Company. Capitalizing on the micro-brewery trend so popular elsewhere, Capitol City is the first brewery to operate in the District since Prohibition. A gleaming copper bar dominates the airy room, with metal steps leading up to where the brews are actually made. ⊠ *1100 New York Ave. NW,* ☎ *202/628–2222.* ☉ *Mon.–Sat. 11 AM–2 AM, Sun. 11 AM–midnight.*

Champions. Walls covered with jerseys, pucks, bats, and balls, and the evening's big game on the big-screen TV—this popular Georgetown establishment is a sports lover's oasis. Ballpark-style food enhances the mood. ⊠ *1206 Wisconsin Ave. NW,* ☎ *202/965–4005.* ☉ *Mon.–Thurs. 5 PM–2 AM, Fri. 5 PM–3 AM, Sat. 11:30 AM–3 AM, Sun. 11:30 AM–2 AM. 1-drink minimum Fri. and Sat. after 10 PM.*

Dubliner. Snug paneled rooms, thick Guinness, and nightly live entertainment make Washington's premier Irish pub popular among Capitol Hill staffers. ⊠ *520 N. Capitol St. NW,* ☎ *202/737–3773.* ☉ *Sun.–Thurs. 11 AM–1:30 AM, Fri.–Sat. 11 AM–2:30 AM.*

15 Mins. A college-age clientele ventures downtown to enjoy the funky decorations, tiny dance floor, progressive music, and black lights that bathe the back room in an eerie, purplish glow. Blues bands, local new music bands, and alternative music heroes such as Eugene Chadbourne and Marc Ribot play at the club or in the adjacent Rothschild's Cafeteria. As for the bar's unusual name, that's how long artist Andy Warhol predicted everyone would be famous in the future: 15 Mins. ⊠ *1030 15th St. NW,* ☎ *202/408–1855.* ▣ *Cover charge.* ☉ *Mon.–Tues. 5 PM–2 AM, Wed.–Thurs. noon–2 AM, Fri. noon–3 AM, Sat. 8 PM–3 AM.*

Food for Thought. Lots of Birkenstock sandals, natural fibers, and activist conversation give this Dupont Circle lounge and restaurant (vegetarian and organic meat) a '60s coffeehouse feel. Nightly folk music completes the picture. ⊠ *1738 Connecticut Ave. NW,* ☎ *202/797–1095.* ☉ *Mon.–Thurs. 11:30 AM–12:30 AM (closed Mon. 3–5), Fri. 11:30 AM–1:30 AM, Sat. noon–1:30 AM, Sun. 4 PM–12:30 AM.*

Hawk 'n' Dove. A friendly neighborhood bar in a neighborhood coincidentally dominated by the Capitol building, Hawk 'n' Dove's regulars include politicos, lobbyists, and well-behaved Marines from a nearby barracks. ⊠ *329 Pennsylvania Ave. SE,* ☎ *202/543–3300.* ☉ *Sun.–Thurs. 10 AM–2 AM, Fri. and Sat. 10 AM–3 AM.*

Sign of the Whale. The best hamburger in town is available at the bar of a well-known post-preppie/neo-yuppie haven. ⊠ *1825 M St. NW,* ☎ *202/785–1110.* ☉ *Sun.–Thurs. 11:30 AM–2 AM, Fri. and Sat. 11:30 AM–3 AM.*

Cabarets

Capitol Steps. The musical political satire of the Capitol Steps, a group of current and former Hill staffers, is presented on Friday and Saturday at Chelsea's, a Georgetown night-club, and occasionally at other spots around town. ⊠ *1055 Thomas Jefferson St. NW; Chelsea's,* ☎ *202/298–8222; Capitol Steps, 703/683–8330.* ▨ *Cover charge.* ☉ *Fri. at 8 and Sat. at 7:30 most weeks. Reservations required.*

Gross National Product. After years of spoofing Republican administrations with such shows as *BushCapades* and *Man Without a Contra,* then aiming its barbs at the Democrats in *Clintoons,* the irreverent comedy troupe Gross National Product was most recently performing *On the Dole.* GNP stages its shows at Arena Stage's Old Vat Theater and at the Bayou in Georgetown. ☎ *202/783–7212 (GNP) for location and reservations, which are advised.* ▨ *Ticket charge.* ☉ *Shows Fri. 8 PM and Sat. 8 and 10 PM.*

Comedy Clubs

Comedy Café. Local and national comics appear at the Comedy Café in the heart of downtown. Wednesday is open-mike night; Thursday is local talent; on Friday and Saturday name comedians headline. ⊠ *1520 K St. NW,* ☎ *202/638–5653.* ▨ *Cover charge.* ☉ *Thurs. at 8:30; Fri. 8:30 and 10:30; Sat. 7, 9, and 11.*

Garvin's Comedy Clubs. Garvin's is one of the oldest names in comedy in Washington and pioneered the practice of organizing comedy nights in suburban hotels. ⊠ *Westpark Hotel, 8401 Westpark Dr., Tysons Corner, VA.* ☉ *Fri. at 9, Sat. 8 and 10.* ⊠ *Augie's Restaurant, I–395 and S. Glebe Rd., Arlington, VA.* ☉ *Fri. and Sat. at 9. For both places,* ☎ *202/872–8880 (information and reservations, which are required).* ▨ *Cover charge and drink minimum.*

Improv. A new heavyweight on the Washington comedy scene, the Improv is descended from the club that sparked the stand-up boomlet in New York City and across the country. Name headliners are common. ⊠ *1140 Connecticut Ave. NW,* ☎ *202/296–7008.* ▨ *Cover charge and 2-item (not* *necessarily drinks) minimum.* ⊙ *Sun.–Thurs. at 8:30, Fri. and Sat. 8:30 and 10:30.*

Dance Clubs

Chelsea's. Should a dance like the *lambada* ever again bubble up from South America, you'll find it at Chelsea's, an elegant Georgetown club near the C&O Canal. On Monday, there is Ethiopian music; Wednesday is world music night; hot Latin acts appear Thursday through Saturday; it's Persian music on Wednesday and Sunday. ✉ *1055 Thomas Jefferson St. NW,* ☎ *202/298–8222.* 🎫 *Cover charge Fri. and Sat.* ⊙ *Wed., Thurs., and Sun. 9:30 PM–2 AM, Fri. and Sat. 9:30 PM–4 AM.*

Fifth Column. A trendy, well-dressed crowd waits in line to dance to the latest releases from London and Europe on three floors of a disco that's actually a converted bank. Avant-garde art installations change every six months. ✉ *915 F St. NW,* ☎ *202/393–3632.* 🎫 *Cover charge.* ⊙ *Mon. 9 PM–2 AM, Wed. and Thurs. 10 PM–2 AM, Fri. and Sat. 10 PM–3 AM.*

Kilimanjaro. Deep in ethnically diverse Adams-Morgan, Kilimanjaro specializes in "international" music from the Caribbean and Africa. Every Thursday there's a local reggae band, and there are occasional weekend shows. ✉ *1724 California St. NW,* ☎ *202/328–3838.* 🎫 *Cover charge.* ⊙ *Wed.–Thurs. 5 PM–2 AM, Fri. 5 PM–4:30 AM, Sat. 8 PM–4 AM, Sun. 6 PM–2 AM.*

Ritz. Near the FBI Building is a downtown nightclub popular with the black professional crowd. The Ritz has five separate rooms of music, with DJs spinning everything from Top 40 and reggae in "Club Matisse" to house music in the upstairs "Freezone." ✉ *919 E St. NW,* ☎ *202/638–2582. Jacket and tie Fri. and Sat. AE, MC, V.* 🎫 *Cover charge.* ⊙ *Wed. 9 PM–2 AM, Fri. 5 PM–3 AM, Sat. 9 PM–3 AM, Sun. 9 PM–2 AM.*

River Club. If you own a pair of spats, they wouldn't look out of place at the River Club, an elegant Georgetown supper club. Its Art Deco decor, like an Erté print come to life, serves as a backdrop for big band music from Doc Scantlin, Washington's answer to Cab Calloway, on Thursday nights. On Wednesday nights, enjoy the sounds of the Admirals. On weekends a DJ spins everything from Motown to big band. This is the perfect place for starring in your own Astaire and Rogers movie. ⊠ *3223 K St. NW,* ☎ *202/333–8118. Jacket and tie.* ⊡ *Cover charge.* ⊗ *Tues.–Thurs. 7 PM–2 AM, Fri. and Sat. 7 PM–3 AM.*

Tracks. A gay club with a large contingent of straight regulars, this warehouse-district disco has one of the largest dance floors in town and stays open late. ⊠ *1111 1st St. SE,* ☎ *202/488–3320.* ⊡ *Cover charge.* ⊗ *Thurs. 9 PM–4 AM, Fri. 8 PM–5 AM, Sat. 8 PM–6 AM, Sun. 4 PM–8 PM (tea dance) and 8 PM–4 AM.*

Zei. The latest attempt to be as hip as the Big Apple, Zei (pronounced "zee") is a New York–style dance club in a former electric power substation. It wants to attract "young, upscale politically aware women and men" with the relentless thump of Euro-Pop dance music and a design that includes a wall of television sets peering down on the proceedings. ⊠ *1415 Zei Alley NW (14th St. between H and I Sts. NW),* ☎ *202/842–2445. No tennis shoes.* ⊡ *Cover charge.* ⊗ *Wed. and Thurs. 10 PM–2 AM, Fri. and Sat. 10 PM–3 AM (call for occasional weeknight events).*

Jazz Clubs

Blues Alley. The restaurant turns out Creole cooking, while cooking on stage are such nationally known performers as Charlie Byrd and Ramsey Lewis. You can come for just the show, but those who come for a meal get better seats. ⊠ *Rear 1073 Wisconsin Ave. NW,* ☎ *202/337–4141.* ⊡ *Cover charge and $7 food/drink minimum.* ⊗ *Sun.–Thurs. 6 PM–midnight, Fri. and Sat. 6 PM–2 AM. Shows at 8 and 10, plus occasional midnight shows Fri. and Sat.*

One Step Down. Low-ceilinged, intimate, and boasting the best jazz jukebox in town, One Step Down is a small club that books talented local artists and the occasional national act. Live music is presented Thursday–Monday. ⊠ *2517 Pennsylvania Ave. NW,* ☎ *202/331–8863.* ⊡ *Cover charge and minimum.* ⊗ *Mon.–Thurs. 10 AM–2 AM, Fri. 10 AM–3 AM, Sat. noon–3 AM, Sun. noon–2 AM.*

Takoma Station Tavern. In the shadow of the Metro stop that lends its name, the Takoma Station Tavern hosts such local favorites as Marshall Keys and Keith Killgo, with the occasional nationally known artist stopping by to jam. The jazz happy hours starting at 6:30 Wednesday through Friday pack the joint. There's reggae on Sundays. ⊠ *6914 4th St. NW*, ☎ *202/829–1999. No sneakers or athletic wear.* ☉ *Sun.–Thurs. 4 PM–2 AM, Fri. and Sat. 4 PM–3 AM.*

Rock, Pop, and Rhythm and Blues Clubs

Bayou. In Georgetown, underneath the Whitehurst Freeway, the Bayou is a Washington fixture that showcases national acts on weeknights and local talent on weekends. Bands cover rock in all its permutations: pop rock, hard rock, soft rock, new rock, and classic rock. Tickets are available at the door or through TicketMaster. ⊠ *3135 K St. NW*, ☎ *202/333–2897.* ▨ *Cover charge.* ☉ *Generally open daily 8 PM–2 AM.*

Grog and Tankard. A college-age crowd downs cheap pitchers of beer while listening to exuberant local bands in the Grog and Tankard, a small, comfortably disheveled night spot. ⊠ *2408 Wisconsin Ave. NW*, ☎ *202/333–3114.* ▨ *Cover charge after 9 PM.* ☉ *Sun.–Thurs. 5 PM–2 AM, Fri.–Sat. 5 PM–3 AM.*

9:30 Club. 9:30 is a trendy club booking an eclectic mix of local, national, and international artists, most of whom play what used to be known as "new wave" music. Get tickets at the door or through TicketMaster. ⊠ *815 V St. NW*, ☎ *202/393–0930.* ▨ *Cover charge.* ☉ *Hrs vary according to shows but generally open Sun.–Thurs. 7:30 PM-midnight, Fri.–Sat. 9 PM–2 AM.*

6 Shopping

By
Deborah
Papier

Updated
by Bruce
Walker

KITCHENWARE AS OBJETS D'ART . . .
American and European antiques . . .
love beads and diamonds—D.C. has
something for shoppers of every stripe. It wasn't always so.
Once shopping here meant a trek to one of the suburban
shopping malls offering far more than what could be found
in town. Visiting Bloomingdale's, Nordstrom, or Macy's
still means going to Montgomery Mall or White Flint Mall
in Bethesda, Maryland (the latter near the White Flint
Metro), the twin megamalls in Tysons Corner, Virginia
(reachable by bus but not subway), or the Fashion Centre
mall at Pentagon City (Metro: Pentagon City). In recent
years, however, the city's own shopping scene has been revitalized. Although some longtime retailers have gone
bankrupt, many of the remaining department stores have
upgraded both their facilities and their merchandise. Many
of the smaller one-of-a-kind shops have managed to survive urban renewal, designer boutiques are increasing, and
interesting specialty shops and minimalls are popping up
all over town. Weekdays downtown, street vendors offer
a funky mix of jewelry, brightly patterned ties, buyer-be-
ware watches, sunglasses, and African-inspired clothing, accessories, and art. Of course, T-shirts and Capital City
souvenirs are always in plentiful supply, especially on the
streets ringing *the* Mall.

Store hours vary greatly. Play it safe. Call ahead. In general, Georgetown stores are open late and on Sunday;
stores downtown that cater to office workers close at 6 PM
and may not be open at all on Saturday or Sunday. Some
stores extend their hours on Thursday.

Sales tax is 6%; major credit cards are accepted virtually
everywhere.

Shopping Districts

Adams-Morgan. Scattered among the dozens of Latin,
Ethiopian, and Caribbean restaurants in this most bohemian of Washington neighborhoods are a score of the city's
most eccentric shops. If quality is what you seek, it's a

minefield; tread cautiously. Still, for the bargain hunter it's great fun. A word of caution—call ahead to verify hours. Adams-Morganites are often not clock-watchers, but you can be sure a weekend afternoon stroll will find a good representation of the shops open and a great few hours of browsing. Most of the shops are on 18th Street NW, between Columbia Road and California Avenue.

Chevy Chase Pavilion. Across from Mazza Gallerie, a major shopping district in the Capitol, is the newer, similarly upmarket Chevy Chase Pavilion. Its exclusive women's clothing stores include Joan & David and Steilmann European Selection (which carries Karl Lagerfeld's sportier KL line). Other specialty shops of note here are the Pottery Barn, the National Cathedral Museum Shop, and Country Road Australia. ⊠ *5335 Wisconsin Ave. NW,* ☎ *202/686–5335.*

Dupont Circle. You might call Dupont Circle a working-class version of Georgetown—blue collar instead of blue blood, not as well kept, with more apartment buildings than houses. But make no mistake: This is one of Washington's most vibrant neighborhoods, with a lively mix of shops and restaurants. The street scene here is grittier than Georgetown's, with fewer teens and older shoppers and more twentysomethings and thirtysomethings.

Eastern Market. As the Capitol Hill area has become gentrified, additional unique shops and boutiques have sprung up in the neighborhood. Many are clustered around the 1873 building known as Eastern Market. Inside are produce and meat counters, plus the Market Five art gallery; outside are a farmer's market (on Saturdays) and a flea market (on weekends). Across 7th Street are Mission Traders (imported handicrafts), Antiques on the Hill (primarily furniture), and Forecast (women's clothing). ⊠ *7th and C Sts. SE, 1 block north of Eastern Market Metro.*

Fashion Centre at Pentagon City. Just across the river in Virginia, a 10-minute ride on the Metro from downtown, is a four-story mall (including food court) with Macy's at one end and Nordstrom at the other. In between are such shops as Liz Claiborne and the Coach Store. ⊠ *1100 S. Hayes St., Arlington, VA,* ☎ *703/415–2400.*

Washington Shopping

Betsy Fisher, **24**

Britches of Georgetown, **21**

Brooks Brothers, **33**

Burberrys, **27**

Chanel Boutique, **40**

Chapters, **37**

Chenonceau Antiques, **8**

Cherishables, **14**

Cheshire Cat, **5**

Chevy Chase Pavilion (shopping center), **4**

Church's, **34**

Eastern Market, **52**

Fahrney's, **39**

Fashion Centre at Pentagon City, **42**

Filene's Basement, **31**

Hecht's, **44**

Indian Craft Shop, **41**

J. Press, **30**

John B. Adler, **38**

Kemp Mill Music, **16, 32**

Kismet Wearable Art, **10**

Kid's Closet, **26**

Kobos, **9**

Kramerbooks, **15**

Lammas Books, **17**

Lord & Taylor, **2**

Marston Luce, **23**

Mazza Gallerie (shopping center), **3**

Moon, Blossoms and Snow, **51**

Music Box Center, **47**
Mystery Books, **6**
Olsson's Books & Records, **19, 45, 48**
Pampillonia Jewelers, **22**
Pavilion at the Old Post Office (shopping center) **46**

Retrospective, **11**
Rizik Bros., **35**
Saks Fifth Avenue, **1**
Second Story Books, **18**
Serenade Record Shop, **28**
Shoe Scene, **25**

The Shops at National Place (shopping center), **43**
Skynear and Company, **12**
Tiny Jewel Box, **29**
Tower Records, **36**
Trover Books, **50**
Uniform, **7**

Union Station (shopping center), **49**
Vertigo Books, **20**
Yawa, **13**

Georgetown. Georgetown remains Washington's favorite shopping area. Though Georgetown is not on a subway line, and parking is impossible, people still flock here. The attraction (aside from the lively street scene) is the profusion of specialty shops in a charming, historic neighborhood. In addition to tony antiques, elegant crafts, and high-style shoe and clothing boutiques, the area offers wares that attract students and other less-well-heeled shoppers: books, music, and fashions from such popular chain stores as the Gap and Benetton.

Georgetown Park. The hub of Georgetown is the intersection of Wisconsin Avenue and M Street, with most of the stores lying to the east and west on M Street and to the north on Wisconsin. Near that intersection is Georgetown Park (⊠ 3222 M St. NW, ☎ 202/298–5577), a three-level mall that looks like a Victorian ice-cream parlor inside. The pricey clothing and accessory boutiques and ubiquitous chain stores (such as Victoria's Secret) in the posh mall draw international tourists in droves. Next door to the mall is a branch of New York's premier gourmet food store, Dean & Deluca (⊠ 3276 M St. NW, ☎ 202/342–2500).

Mazza Galleria. A major shopping district is on upper Wisconsin Avenue straddling the Maryland border. Called the Mazza Galleria, the four-level mall is anchored by the ritzy Neiman Marcus department store and a Filene's Basement. Its other stores include Williams-Sonoma's kitchenware and Laura Ashley Home. Other department stores are close by: Lord & Taylor and Saks Fifth Avenue (☞ Department Stores, *below*). ⊠ *5300 Wisconsin Ave. NW, ☎ 202/966–6114.*

Shops at National Place. The Shops takes up three levels, one of which is devoted to food stands. Although mainly youth-oriented (this is a good place to drop off teenagers weary of the Smithsonian and more in the mood to buy T-shirts), The Limited, Victoria's Secret, and The Sharper Image have stores here, too. ⊠ *By Metro Center, 13th and F Sts. NW, ☎ 202/783–9090.*

Pavilion at the Old Post Office. The city is justly proud of its Old Post Office Pavilion, a handsome shopping center in a historic building with 19th-century origins. In addition to the 16 food vendors, there are 17 shops, among them

Georgetown Shopping

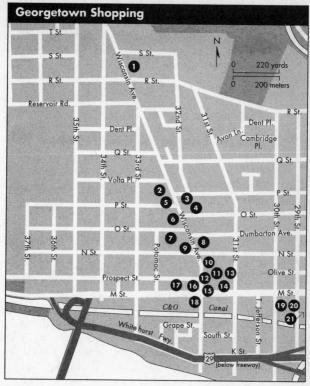

American Hand, **20**

Appalachian Spring, **5**

Betsey Johnson, **8**

Britches Great Outdoors, **15**

Britches of Georgetown, **10**

Chevy Chase Pavilion (shopping center), **4**

Coach Store, **16**

Commander Salamander, **6**

Earl Allen, **14**

Georgetown Antiques Center, **19**

Georgetown Park (mall), **18**

G.K.S. Bush, **21**

HMV Records, **12**

Martin's, **9**

Miller & Arney Antiques, **1**

Old Print Gallery, **13**

Olsson's Books & Records, **11**

Opportunity Shop, **3**

Orpheus Records, **17**

Phoenix, **2**

Susquehanna, **7**

Condor Imports (for South American and African clothing and crafts) and Juggling Capitol (for beginner to expert jugglers). The observation deck in the building's clock tower offers an excellent view of the city. ⊠ *12th St. NW and Pennsylvania Ave.,* ☎ *202/289–4224.*

Union Station. One of the most delightful shopping enclaves in the Capitol, Union Station is resplendent with marble floors and gilded, vaulted ceilings. It's now both a working train station and a mall with three levels of stores—one with food stands and a cinema multiplex—and, appropriately, the Great Train Store, which offers train memorabilia and toy versions from the inexpensive to four-digit Swiss models. The east hall, reminiscent of London's Covent Garden, is filled with vendors of expensive and ethnic wares in open stalls. Christmas is an especially pleasant time to shop here. ⊠ *Massachusetts Ave. NE near N. Capitol St.,* ☎ *202/371–9441.*

Department Stores

Filene's Basement. At this mecca for bargain hunters, steep discounts can be had on Christian Dior, Hugo Boss, Burberrys, and other designer men's and women's clothing labels. Off-price apparel, shoes, perfume, and accessories are offered as well. Despite the prices, neither of the Washington branches has a bargain-basement atmosphere. ⊠ *1133 Connecticut Ave. NW,* ☎ *202/872–8430. Metro: Farragut North.* ⊠ *5300 Wisconsin Ave. NW,* ☎ *202/966–0208.*

Hecht's. The main downtown store is bright and spacious, and its sensible groupings and attractive displays of merchandise make shopping relatively easy on the feet and the eyes. The clothes sold here are a mix of conservative and trendy lines, with the men's department assuming increasing importance. Sadly, one of the things that makes Hecht's Hecht's today is that it remains open; all its downtown neighbors—Garfinckel's and Woodward & Lothrop recently, Lansburgh's some years ago—have pulled up stakes. ⊠ *12th and G Sts. NW,* ☎ *202/628–6661.*

Lord & Taylor. Lord & Taylor lets the competition be all things to all people while it focuses on nonutilitarian housewares and classic clothing by such designers as Anne Klein and Ralph Lauren. All clothing is designed and made in the United States. ⊠ *5255 Western Ave. NW,* ☎ *202/362–9600.*

Neiman Marcus. If price is an object, this is definitely not the place to shop, although it's still fun to browse. Headquartered in Dallas, Neiman Marcus caters to customers who value quality above all. The carefully selected merchandise includes couture clothes, furs, precious jewelry, crystal, and silver. ⊠ *Mazza Gallerie, 5300 Wisconsin Ave. NW,* ☎ *202/966–9700.*

Saks Fifth Avenue. Though not technically a Washington department store since it is just over the Maryland line, Saks is nonetheless a Washington institution, with a wide selection of European and American couture clothes. ⊠ *5555 Wisconsin Ave.,* ☎ *301/657–9000.*

Specialty Stores

Antiques and Collectibles

Chenonceau Antiques. The mostly American 19th- and 20th-century pieces on these two floors were selected by a buyer with an exquisite eye. Merchandise includes beautiful 19th-century paisley scarves from India and from Scotland, and 1920s glass lamps. ⊠ *2314 18th St. NW,* ☎ *202/ 667–1651.* ☉ *Fri.–Sun.*

Cherishables. American 18th- and 19th-century furniture and decorative arts are the featured attractions at Cherishables, with emphasis on the Federal period. ⊠ *1608 20th St. NW,* ☎ *202/785–4087.*

Georgetown Antiques Center. The center, in a Victorian town house, has two dealers who share space: Cherub Gallery (☎ 202/337–2224) specializes in Art Nouveau and Art Deco, and **Michael Getz Antiques** (☎ 202/338–3811) sells fireplace equipment and silverware. ⊠ *2918 M St. NW.*

G. K. S. Bush. G. K. S. Bush sells formal 18th- and early 19th-century American furniture and related works. ⊠ *2828 Pennsylvania Ave. NW,* ☎ *202/965–0653.*

Marston Luce. Focusing on American folk art, including quilts, weather vanes, and hooked rugs, Marston Luce also carries home and garden furnishings, primarily American, but some English and French as well. ⊠ *1314 21st St. NW,* ☎ *202/775–9460.*

Miller & Arney Antiques. English, American, and European furniture and accessories from the 18th and early 19th centuries give Miller & Arney Antiques a museum gallery air. Oriental porcelain adds splashes of color. ⊠ *1737 Wisconsin Ave. NW,* ☎ *202/338–2369.*

Old Print Gallery. The Capitol's largest collection of old prints and maps (including Washingtoniana) is housed in the Old Print Gallery. ⊠ *1220 31st St. NW,* ☎ *202/965–1818.*

Opportunity Shop of the Christ Child Society. A Georgetown thrift shop, Opportunity Shop sells vintage clothing and good-quality household goods. Consigned fine antiques at moderate prices are available on the second floor ⊠ *1427 Wisconsin Ave. NW,* ☎ *202/333–6635.*

Retrospective. A small shop crammed with high-quality furniture and accessories, mostly from the '40s and '50s, Retrospective is a place where you can still buy the princess phone that lit up your nightstand in 1962 and the plates your mother served her meat loaf on. ⊠ *2324 18th St. NW,* ☎ *202/483–8112.*

Susquehanna. The largest antiques shop in Georgetown, Susquehanna specializes in American furniture and paintings. ⊠ *3216 O St. NW,* ☎ *202/333–1511.*

Uniform. The best of the vintage clothing and household accessories shops in the Adams-Morgan neighborhood, Uniform has a vast assortment from the '50s and '60s: piles of fatigue, Nehru, and tie-died shirts, Sergeant Pepper jackets, navy pea coats, and all sorts of other formerly ordinary stuff now prized as icons of a bygone era. You'll also find lava lamps, pillbox hats, feathered mules with Lucite heels, and plateware that could have been props for the Jetsons. ⊠ *2407 18th St. NW,* ☎ *202/483–4577.*

Books

Chapters. A "literary bookstore," Chapters eschews cartoon collections and diet guides, filling its shelves instead with serious contemporary fiction, classics, and poetry. ⊠ *1512 K St. NW,* ☎ *202/347–5495.*

Cheshire Cat. This bookstore for children carries a selection of records, cassettes, posters, and books on parenting. ⊠ *5512 Connecticut Ave. NW,* ☎ *202/244–3956.*

Kramerbooks. Open 24 hours on weekends, Kramerbooks shares space with a café that has late-night dining and weekend entertainment. The stock is small but well selected. ⊠ *1517 Connecticut Ave. NW,* ☎ *202/387–1400.*

Lammas Books. A selection of music by women as well as women's and lesbian literature is for sale here. ⊠ *1426 21st St. NW,* ☎ *202/775–8218.*

Mystery Books. Mystery Books has Washington's largest collection of detective, crime, suspense, and spy fiction. They deliver "Crime and Nourishment" gift baskets anywhere in the United States (☎ 800/955–2279). ⊠ *1715 Connecticut Ave. NW,* ☎ *202/483–1600.*

Second Story Books. A mecca for bibliophiles that encourages hours of browsing, this used-books (and records) emporium is located on Dupont Circle. ⊠ *2000 P St. NW,* ☎ *202/659–8884.*

Trover Books. The latest political volumes and out-of-town newspapers are here. ⊠ *221 Pennsylvania Ave. SE,* ☎ *202/ 547–2665.*

Vertigo Books. Just south of Dupont Circle, Vertigo Books emphasizes international politics, world literature, and African-American studies. ⊠ *1337 Connecticut Ave. NW,* ☎ *202/429–9272.*

Yawa. Featuring a large collection of African and African-American fiction and nonfiction, magazines, and children's books, Yawa also sells ethnic jewelry, crafts, and greeting cards. ⊠ *2206 18th St. NW,* ☎ *202/483–6805.*

Children's Clothing and Toys

F.A.O. Schwarz. F.A.O. Schwarz is the most upscale of toy stores, carrying such items as a toy car (a Mercedes, of course) that costs almost as much as the real thing. Among the other imports are stuffed animals (many larger than life), dolls, and children's perfumes. ⊠ *Georgetown Park, 3222 M St. NW,* ☎ *202/342–2285.*

Kid's Closet. The downtown choice for baby clothes and shower gifts, The Kid's Closet also stocks some togs for older children. ⊠ *1226 Connecticut Ave. NW,* ☎ *202/429–9247.*

Crafts and Gifts

American Hand. For one-of-a-kind functional and non-functional pieces by America's foremost ceramic artists, this is a wonderful place. The American Hand also carries limited edition objects for home and office, such as architect-designed dinnerware. ⊠ *2906 M St. NW,* ☎ *202/965–3273.*

Appalachian Spring. Appalachian Spring's two Washington stores sell traditional and contemporary crafts, including quilts, jewelry, weavings, pottery, and blown glass. ⊠ *1415 Wisconsin Ave. NW,* ☎ *202/337–5780;* ⊠ *Union Station,* ☎ *202/682–0505.*

Fahrney's. Starting out as a pen bar in the Willard Hotel, a place to fill your fountain pen before embarking on the day's business, Fahrney's today sells pens in silver, gold, and lacquer by the world's leading manufacturers. ⊠ *1430 G St. NW,* ☎ *202/628–9525.*

Indian Craft Shop. Handicrafts, including jewelry, pottery, sand paintings, weavings, and baskets from a dozen Native American tribes—including Navajo, Pueblo, Zuni, Cherokee, Lakota, and Seminole—are for sale. Items range from inexpensive jewelry (for as little as $6) on up to collector-quality antiques costing $1,000 or more. ⊠ *Dept. of Interior, 1849 C St. NW, Room 1023,* ☎ *202/208–4056.*

Martin's. Martin's is a long-established Georgetown purveyor of china, crystal, and silver. ⊠ *1304 Wisconsin Ave. NW,* ☎ *202/338–6144.*

Moon, Blossoms and Snow. Moon, Blossoms and Snow concentrates on wearable art. In addition to hand-painted, handwoven garments, the store sells contemporary American ceramics, glass, jewelry, and wood. ⊠ *225 Pennsylvania Ave. SE,* ☎ *202/543–8181.*

Music Box Center. An exquisite specialty store, the Music Box Center provides listening opportunities via more than 1,500 music boxes that play 500 melodies. ⊠ *918 F St. NW,* ☎ *202/783–9399.*

Phoenix. The Phoenix sells Mexican crafts, including folk art, silver jewelry, fabrics, and native and contemporary clothing in natural fibers. ⊠ *1514 Wisconsin Ave. NW,* ☎ *202/338–4404.*

Skynear and Company. The owners of Skynear and Company travel the world to find the unusual—and do: an extravagant assortment of rich textiles, furniture, and home accessories for the art of living. ⊠ *2122 18th St. NW,* ☎ *202/797–7160;* ⊠ *Mazza Gallerie, 5300 Wisconsin Ave. NW,* ☎ *202/362–7541.*

Jewelry

Charles Schwartz & Son. A full-service jeweler, Charles Schwartz specializes in precious stones in traditional and modern settings. Fine watches are also offered. ⊠ *Mazza Gallerie, 1213 Connecticut Ave. NW,* ☎ *202/363–5432.*

Pampillonia Jewelers. Traditional designs in 18-karat gold and platinum are found here, including many pieces for men. ⊠ *Mazza Gallerie,* ☎ *202/363–6305;* ⊠ *1213 Connecticut Ave. NW,* ☎ *202/628–6305.*

Tiny Jewel Box. The Tiny Jewel Box features well-chosen estate jewelry, contemporary jewelry, and unique gifts. ⊠ *1143 Connecticut Ave. NW,* ☎ *202/393–2747. Metro: Farragut North.*

Leather Goods

Coach Store. For fine leather, the Coach Store carries a complete (and expensive) line of well-made handbags, briefcases, belts, and wallets. ⊠ *1214 Wisconsin Ave. NW,* ☎ *202/342–1772.*

Georgetown Leather Design. Most of the leather goods in this collection—including jackets, briefcases, wallets, gloves, and handbags—are custom-made for the store. ⊠ *Fashion Centre at Pentagon City, 1100 S. Hayes St., Arlington, VA,* ☎ *703/418–6702.*

Men's Clothing

Britches of Georgetown. Britches carries an extensive selection of traditional but trend-conscious designs in natural fibers. ⊠ *1219 Connecticut Ave. NW,* ☎ *202/347–8994;* ⊠ *1247 Wisconsin Ave. NW,* ☎ *202/338–3330.*

Brooks Brothers. The oldest men's store in America, Brooks Brothers has sold traditional formal and casual clothing since 1818. It is the largest men's specialty store in the area and has a small women's department as well. ⊠ *1840 L St. NW,* ☎ *202/659–4650;* ⊠ *5504 Wisconsin Ave.,* ☎ *301/654–8202.*

J. Press. J. Press was founded in 1902 as a custom shop for Yale University. It is a resolutely traditional clothier: Shetland wool sport coats are a specialty. ⊠ *1801 L St. NW,* ☎ *202/857–0120.*

Men's and Women's Clothing

Britches Great Outdoors. The casual version of Britches of Georgetown, Britches Great Outdoors has filled many Washington closets with rugby shirts and other sportswear. ⊠ *1225 Wisconsin Ave. NW,* ☎ *202/333–3666.*

Burberrys. Burberrys made its reputation with the trench coat, but this British company also manufactures traditional men's and women's apparel. ⊠ *1155 Connecticut Ave. NW,* ☎ *202/463–3000.*

Commander Salamander. As much entertainment as funky shopping—leather, chains, silver skulls—it's open until 10 on weekends. ⊠ *1420 Wisconsin Ave. NW,* ☎ *202/337–2265.*

John B. Adler. A longtime Washington clothier, John B. Adler offers the Ivy League look in suits, sport coats, and formal and casual wear. ⊠ *901 15th St. NW (entrance on I St.),* ☎ *202/842–4432.*

Kobos. A rainbow of clothing and accessories imported from West Africa is for sale at Kobos, plus a small selection of African music. ⊠ *2444 18th St. NW,* ☎ *202/332–9580.*

Music

HMV Records. A new two-story music store in Georgetown, HMV Records specializes in rock but also has a large selection of classical music. ⊠ *1229 Wisconsin Ave. NW,* ☎ *202/333–9292.*

Olsson's Books & Records. Here's a full line of compact discs and cassettes, with a good classical and folk music selection. Hours vary significantly from store to store. ⊠ *1239 Wisconsin Ave. NW,* ☎ *202/338–9544;* ⊠ *1307 19th St. NW,* ☎ *202/785–1133;* ⊠ *1200 F St. NW,* ☎ *202/347–3686;* ⊠ *418 7th St. NW,* ☎ *202/638–7610.*

Orpheus Records. Orpheus Records specializes in new and used jazz and blues records. ⊠ *3249 M St. NW,* ☎ *202/337–7970.*

Serenade Record Shop. A full-catalog music store, the Serenade Record Shop is especially strong in classical music. ⊠ *1800 M St. NW,* ☎ *202/452–0075.*

Tower Records. The 16,000-square-foot Tower Records offers Washington's best selection of music in all categories, plus videos and laser discs. ⊠ *2000 Pennsylvania Ave. NW,* ☎ *202/331–2400;* ⊠ *Rockville, MD,* ☎ *301/468–8901;* ⊠ *Vienna, VA,* ☎ *703/893–6627.*

Shoes

Church's. Church's is an English company whose handmade men's shoes are noted for their comfort and durability. ⊠ *1820 L St. NW,* ☎ *202/296–3366.*

Shoe Scene. The fashionable, moderately priced shoes for women found here are direct imports from Europe. ⊠ *1330 Connecticut Ave. NW,* ☎ *202/659–2194.*

Women's Clothing

Betsey Johnson. This shop sells fanciful frocks for the young and restless. ⊠ *1319 Wisconsin Ave. NW,* ☎ *202/338–4090.*

Betsy Fisher. *Tasteful* is the word that best describes Betsy Fisher's clothing; it appeals to women of all ages. ⊠ *1224 Connecticut Ave. NW,* ☎ *202/785–1975.*

Chanel Boutique. The Willard Hotel annex is where to find goodies from the legendary house of fashion. ⊠ *1455 Pennsylvania Ave. NW,* ☎ *202/638–5055.*

Earl Allen. Catering to the professional woman, Earl Allen offers conservative but distinctive dresses and sportswear, much of it made exclusively for this shop with two locations in the Capitol. ⊠ *3109 M St. NW,* ☎ *202/338–1678;* ⊠ *1825 I St. NW,* ☎ *202/466-3437.*

Khismet Wearable Art. Original fashions and traditional garments designed by Millée Spears, who lived in Ghana, fill colorful Khismet. Spears uses ethnic textiles both for garments suitable for the office and for an evening out. ⊠ *1800 Belmont Rd. NW,* ☎ *202/234-7778.*

Rizik Bros. Rizik Bros. is a Washington institution combining designer clothing and accessories with expert service. The sales staff is trained to find just the right style from the large inventory, and prices are right. Take the elevator up from the northwest corner of Connecticut and L streets. ⊠ *1100 Connecticut Ave. NW,* ☎ *202/223-4050.*

INDEX

A

Acoustic music, *129*
Adams Building, *46*
Adams-Morgan, shopping in, *136–137*
Adams-Morgan/Woodley Park restaurants in, *87, 89, 92–94*
Aditi ✗, *104*
Afterwords (music), *129*
Airfares, *xxi*
Airlines, *xiii*
Airports, *xiii*
travel to and from, *xiii–xiv*
Alexandria, VA, *74–75, 77–80*
Alexandria Archaeology Program, *80*
Alexandria Black History Resource Center, *75*
Alexandria Convention & Visitors Bureau, *79*
American Film Institute, *123*
American Hand (shop), *146*
American Red Cross, *29*
American Victoriana collection, *12–13*
Anacostia Museum, *80*
Antiques, *143–144*
Antiques on the Hill (shop), *137*
Appalachian Spring (shop), *146*
Aquarium, *50–51*
Arena Stage (theater), *127*
Arlington National Cemetery, *80–81*
Armed Forces Concert Series, *126*
Arthur M. Sackler Gallery, *12*
Art Museum of the Americas, *29*
Arts, *121–128*
dance, *122*
film, *123*
music, *124–126*
opera, *126–127*
theater, *127–128*
tickets, *122*
Arts and Industries Building, *12–13*
Athenaeum, *75*
ATMs, *xvii, xxvi*

B

Bacon, Henry, *23*
Ballet, *122*
Barnes, Edward Larabee, *48*
Bars and lounges, *129–130*
Bartholdi, Frédéric-Auguste, *40*
Bartholdi Fountain, *40*
Bayou (club), *134*
Beales family, *31*
Bellevue Hotel, *108*
Ben's Chili Bowl ✗, *105*
Bethune Museum and Archives, *81*
Betsy Fisher (shop), *149*
Birchmere (music), *129*
Bison Bridge, *65*
Bistro Français ✗, *103–104*
Black History National Recreation Trail, *xix*
Black National Historic Site, *81–82*
Blair House, *29*
Blue Room, White House, *38*
Blues Alley (jazz club), *133*
B'nai B'rith Klutznick Museum, *65*
Boat tours, *xviii*
Bombay Club ✗, *98*
Bookstores, *144–145*
Booth, John Wilkes, *51*
Braddock, General, *77*
Brick Capitol, *42*
Brickskeller (bar), *129*
Britches of Georgetown (shop), *148*
British travelers, tips for, *xvii, xxiii, xxiv, xxvi*
Brooks Brothers (shop), *148*
Brown, John, *79*
Brumidi, Constantino, *43*
Bukom Cafe, *89*
Bulfinch, Charles, *42*
Burberrys (shop), *148*
Bureau of Engraving and Printing, *13*
Burma ✗, *96–97*
Burnham, Daniel, *49*
Bus travel, *xiii–xiv, xxi–xxii*
tours, *xviii, xix*
Bush, George, *38*
Business hours, *xxii*

C

C & O Canal, 59
Cabarets, 131
Café Asia ✕, 97
Café Nema ✕, 105
Capitol cafeteria, 44
Capitol City Brewing Company (bar), 129
Capitol grounds, 40, 42–44
Capitol Hill, 39–40, 42–49
guided tours, 43
hotels, 107–108
restaurants, 88, 94–95
Captain's Row, 75
Car rental, xv, xxii–xxiii
Car travel, xxiv
Carlton ☎, 109
Carlyle House, 75, 77
Carroll, John, 62
Carter Barron Amphitheater, 126
"The Castle," 21
Challenger, 44
Chamber music, 124–125
Champions (bar), 130
Chanel Boutique (shop), 149
Chapters (bookstore), 144–145
Chelsea's (dance club), 132
Chenonceau Antiques (shop), 143
Cherishables (shop), 143
Cherry Blossom Festival, 26
Cherry trees, 26
Chesapeake & Ohio Canal, 59
Cheshire Cat (bookstore), 145
Chevy Chase Pavilion (shopping area), 137
Children, activities for, 13, 17, 19–20, 26, 49, 59, 82–83, 84
Chinatown, 86
Choral Arts Society, 125
Choral music, 125
Christ Church, 77
"Church of the Presidents," 36
Churches
Christ Church, 77
St. John's Episcopal Church, 36
Church's (shop), 149
Citronelle ✕, 104
City Post Office, 47
City Lights of China ✕, 100–101
Civil War exhibition, 56
Clark Collection, 31

Clay, Henry, 31
Cleveland, Grover, 57
Climate, xxvii–xxviii
Clinton, Bill, 38
Clothes, shopping, 148
Cluss, Adolph, 13
Coach Store, 147
Cockburn, George, 42
Comedy Café (comedy club), 131
Comedy clubs, 131
Committee to Promote Washington, xx
Concert Hall, 121
Concert halls, 124
Confederate Statue, 77
Congressional Research Service, 45
Constitution Gardens, 22–23
Corcoran, William Wilson, 35
Corcoran Gallery of Art, 29, 31, 124
Country music, 129
Cox, John, 59
Cox's Row, 59
Crafts and gifts, 146–147
Credit cards, xxvi
Cret, Paul Philippe, 72
Customs and duties, xxiii–xxiv

D

Dance, 122
Dance clubs, 132–133
Dance Place (studio theater), 122
Dandy, xvii
DAR Constitution Hall, 124
DAR Museum, 33–34
Dean & Deluca (shop), 140
Decatur, Stephen, 31
Decatur House, 31–32
Dentists, xvi
Department of Agriculture, 13
Department of Commerce, 50–51
Department of State building, 71–72
Department of the Interior, 32
Department of the Interior Museum, 32
Dinosaur Hall, 20
Diplomatic Reception Rooms, 71
Disabilities & Accessibility, xv–xvi, xxiv
Discovery Room, 20
Doctors, xvi
Dole, Bob and Elizabeth, 74
Douglass, Frederick, 45, 81–82

Downtown
hotels, 108–109, 112–114
restaurants, 86–87, 96–100
Dubliner (bar), 130
Dumbarton Bridge, 65
Dumbarton Oaks, 60, 62
Dupont Circle, 64–65, 67–70
hotels, 114–115
restaurants, 88, 100–102
shopping, 137

E

Earl Allen (shop), 150
East Room, White House, 38
Eastern Market, 137
Eisenhower Theater, 121
Emergencies, *xvi*
Evermay, 62
Executive Mansion, 37
The Exorcist steps, 62

F

Fahrney's (shop), 146
FAO Schwarz (shop), 145–146
Fashion Centre at Pentagon City, 137
Federal Reserve Building, 72
Federal Triangle, 50
15 Mins. (bar), 130
Fifth Column (dance club), 132
Filene's Basement (department store), 140, 142
Film, 123
Flagg, Ernest, 29
Foggy Bottom, 71–74
hotels, 118–119
Folger Shakespeare Library, 44, 124–125
Folk music, 129
Fondo Del Sol Visual Art and Media Center, 67
Food for Thought (bar), 130
Ford's Theatre, 51, 127
Forecast (shop), 137
Fort Dupont Summer Theater, 126
Four Seasons Hotel, 116
Francis Scott Key Memorial Bridge, 62
Francis Scott Key Memorial Park, 62
Franciscan Monastery and Gardens, 81
Frederick Douglass National Historic Site, 81–82

Frederick Douglass Townhouse, 45
Freed, James Ingo, 22
Freer, Charles L., 16
Freer Gallery of Art, 13, 16
French, Daniel Chester, 24
Friendship Arch, 51
Friendship Fire Company, 77

G

Gadsby's Tavern Museum, 77–78
Gala Hispanic Theatre, 127
Galileo ✕, 98
Gallatin, Albert, 47
Garfield, James, 37
Garvin's Comedy Clubs, 131
Gay and lesbian travelers, hints for, *xvi*
George Washington Masonic National Memorial, 78
George Washington University, 72–73
Georgetown, 58–60, 62–64
hotels, 116–117
restaurants, 87, 102–105
shopping, 140
Georgetown Antiques Center, 143
Georgetown Café ✕, 102–103
Georgetown Estates, 62
Georgetown Suites ⊡, 116–117
Georgetown Leather Design (shop), 147
Georgetown Park (mall), 140
Georgetown University, 62–63
Georgia Brown's ✕, 99–100
Gerard's Place ✕, 98
Gilbert, Cass, 48
G.K.S. Bush (shop), 143
Grant, Ulysses S., 45
Grant Memorial, 45
Great Train Store, 142
Green Room, White House, 38
Grog and Tankard (club), 134

H

Hall of Flags and Heroes, 32
Hall of Presidents, 56
Hall of Remembrance, 22
Hawk 'n' Dove (bar), 130
Hay-Adams Hotel, 109
Hecht's (department store), 142

Henley Park Hotel, *113*
Heurich Mansion, *67–68*
Hibiscus Café ✕, *103*
Hillwood Museum, *82*
Hirshhorn Museum, *16, 123*
Historical Society of Washington, D.C., *67*
History, *4*
Hoban, James, *37*
Holiday Inn Capital Hill 🏨, *108–109*
Hope Diamond, *20*
Hospital, *xvi*
Hotels, *xvii, 107–109, 112–119*
Bellevue Hotel, *108*
Capitol Hilton, *108–109*
Carlton, *109*
Four Seasons Hotel, *116*
Georgetown Suites, *116–117*
Hay-Adams Hotel, *109*
Henley Park Hotel, *113*
Holiday Inn Capitol Hill, *108*
Hotel Sofitel Washington, *114–115*
Hotel Tabard Inn, *115*
Hotel Washington, *113–114*
Jefferson Hotel, *109, 112*
Kalorama Guest House, *117*
Latham Hotel, *116*
Madison Hotel, *112*
Morrison-Clark Inn Hotel, *114*
Normandy Inn, *117–118*
Omni Shoreham Hotel, *117*
Park Hyatt, *118*
Phoenix Park Hotel, *107–108*
Ritz-Carlton, *114*
River Inn, *119*
Stouffer Renaissance Mayflower, *112*
Washington Courtyard by Marriott, *115*
Washington Hilton and Towers, *115*
Watergate Hotel, *74, 118–119*
Willard Inter-Continental, *112–113*
Hotel Sofitel Washington, *114–115*
Hotel Tabard Inn, *115*
Hotel Washington, *113–114*
House of Representatives, *43–44*
House of the Americas, *32*
Houses, on the Hill, *44*

I

I Ricchi ✕, *99*
Ice skating, *20–21, 35*
Imani Café ✕, *95*

Improv (comedy club), *131–132*
Indian Craft Shop, *146*
Inlet Bridge, *26*
Islander ✕, *93–94*
Insurance, *xvi–xvii, xxii–xxiii, xxvi*
InterAmerican Development Bank Cultural Center, *51–52*

J

J. Edgar Hoover Federal Bureau of Investigation Building, *52*
Jackson, Andrew, *37*
Jacqueline Kennedy Rose Garden, *38*
James Garfield Memorial, *45*
James Madison Building, *46*
Jazz clubs, *133–134*
Jefferson, Thomas, *33, 37, 45*
Jefferson Building, *46*
Jefferson Hotel, *109, 112*
Jefferson Memorial, *23*
Jewelry, *147*
Joan & David (shop), *137*
John B. Adler (shop), *148*
John F. Kennedy Center for the Performing Arts, *73, 121–122*
Johnson, Philip, *121*
Juggling Capitol (shop), *142*

K

Kalorama Guest House 🏨, *117*
Kennedy, John F., *50, 53, 73, 80*
grave of, 80
Key (movie theater), *123*
Key, Francis Scott, *62*
Key Bridge, *62*
Khismet Wearable Art (shop), *150*
Kid's Closet (store), *146*
Kilimanjaro (dance club), *132*
King, Martin Luther, *24, 50, 52*
Kobos (shop), *148*
Korean War Veterans Memorial, *24*
Kramerbooks (shop), *145*

L

La Brasserie ✕, *95*
La Chaumière ✕, *103*
La Colline ✕, *95*
La Fourchette ✕, *92*
Lafayette Square, *33*
Lammas Books (shop), *145*
Lannuier, Charles-Honoré, *38*

Latham Hotel, *116*
Latrobe, Benjamin, *31, 36, 42*
Laura Ashley Home (shop), *140*
Layman, Christopher, *63*
Le Lion D'Or ✕, *97*
Leather goods, *147*
Lee, Richard Henry, *78*
Lee, Robert E., *75, 77, 79*
  boyhood home of, 75
Lee Corner, *78*
Lee-Fendall House, *78*
L'Enfant, Pierre, *24, 33, 36, 37, 40, 50*
Library of Congress, *45–46*
Limousines, *xiv*
Lin, Maya Ying, *26–27*
Lincoln, Abraham, *42, 51*
  Ford's Theatre and, 51
  portrait of, 39
Lincoln Memorial, *23–24*
Lisner Auditorium, *124*
Lloyd House, *78*
Lockkeeper's house, *24, 26*
Lodging, *xvii, 107–109, 112–119*
Logan Sapphire, *20*
Lord & Taylor (department store), *140, 142–143*
Louisiana Purchase, *47*
Luggage, *xvi–xvii*
Lyceum, *78*

M

Madison, Dolley, *34*
Madison, James, *34, 36*
Maison Blanche ✕, *97–98*
The Mall, *9, 12–13, 16–22*
Mama Ayesha's Restaurant ✕, *93*
Mango's ✕, *105*
Marrakesh ✕, *99*
Marston Luce (shop), *143–144*
Martin Luther King Memorial Library, *52*
Martin's (shop), *146*
Mary Pickford Theater, *123*
Mazza Gallerie (shopping mall), *140*
McMillan Commission, *48–49*
Mellon, Andrew, *17–18*
Memorial Continental Hall, *33–34*
Memorial to Robert A. Taft, *46–47*
Meskerem ✕, *89, 92*
Metro, *xiv, xix–xx, xxvii*

Miller & Arney Antiques, *144*
Mills, Robert, *36*
Mineral and gem collection, *20*
Mission Traders (shop), *137*
Money matters, *xvii, xxvi*
Monocle ✕, *94*
Monroe, James, *38*
Monuments, *22–24, 26–28*
Moon, Blossoms and Snow (shop), *146*
Morrison-Clark Inn Hotel, *114*
Mullett, Alfred B., *34*
Museums
  Anacostia Museum, 80
  Art Museum of the Americas, 29
  Arthur M. Sackler Gallery, 12
  Arts and Industries Building, 12
  B'nai B'rith Klutznick Museum, 65
  Capital Children's Museum, 91
  Corcoran Gallery of Art, 29, 31, 124
  DAR Museum, 33–34
  Department of the Interior Museum, 32
  Freer Gallery of Art, 13, 16
  Gadsby's Tavern Museum, 86
  Hillwood Museum, 82
  Hirshhorn Museum, 16
  National Air and Space Museum, 17
  National Building Museum, 57
  National Gallery of Art, 17–18, 124
  National Museum of African Art, 18
  National Museum of American Art, 53
  National Museum of American History, 19
  National Museum of American Jewish Military History, 68
  National Museum of Natural History, 19–20
  National Portrait Gallery, 55
  National Postal Museum, 47
  Phillips Collection, 68–69, 125
  Renwick Gallery, 35–36
  Stabler-Leadbeater Apothecary, 79
  Textile Museum, 69–70
  United States Holocaust Memorial Museum, 22
  Washington Dolls' House and Toy Museum, 84
Music, *124–127*
Music Box Center (shop), *147*
Mystery Books (shop), *145*

N

National Academy of Sciences, *125*
National Air and Space Museum, *17*
National Aquarium, *50–51*
National Archives, *52–53*
National Building Museum, *57*
National Gallery of Art, *17–18, 124*
National Gallery Orchestra, *124*
National Geographic Society's Explorer's Hall, *68, 123*
National Monument Society, *27*
National Museum of African Art, *18*
National Museum of American Art, *53*
National Museum of American Jewish Military History, *68*
National Museum of Natural History, *19–20*
National Museum of Women in the Arts, *53*
National Park Service, *xx*
National Portrait Gallery, *53*
National Postal Museum, *47*
National Sculpture Garden Ice Rink, *20–21*
National Shrine of the Immaculate Conception, *82*
National Symphony Orchestra, *125*
National Theatre, *127*
National Zoological Park, *82–83*
Neiman Marcus (department store), *140, 143*
New Heights ✕, *93*
Nightlife, *128–134*
acoustic, folk, country, *129*
bars and lounges, *129–130*
cabarets, *131*
comedy clubs, *131–132*
dance clubs, *132–133*
jazz clubs, *133–134*
rock, pop, and rhythm and blues clubs, *134*
9:30 Club (rock club), *134*
Nixon, Richard M., *52, 74*
Nora ✕, *102*
Normandy Inn 🖫, *117–118*
Northwest, hotels in, *117–118*

O

Octagon House, *34*
Old Downtown and Federal Triangle, *50–53, 56–57*

Old Ebbitt Grill ✕, *96*
Old Executive Office Building, *34–35*
Old Patent Office Building, *53, 56*
Old Presbyterian Meeting House, *79*
Old Print Gallery (shop), *144*
Old Stone House, *63*
Olmsted, Frederick Law, Sr., *40*
Olsson's Books & Records (shop), *149*
Omni Shoreham Hotel, *117*
One Step Down (jazz club), *133*
Opera, *126–127*
Opera House, *121*
Oppenheimer Diamond, *20*
Opportunity Shop of the Christ Child Society, *144*
Orchestral music, *125*
Orpheus Records (shop), *149*
Oswald, Lee Harvey, *53*
Oval Office, White House, *38*

P

The Palm ✕, *96*
Paper currency, printing of, *13*
Park Hyatt 🖫, *118*
Passports, *xvii, xxvi*
Pasta Mia ✕, *92*
Pavilion at the Old Post Office (mall), *140, 142*
Peace Monument, *47*
Pension Building, *57*
Pentagon, *83–84*
Performance Series, *126*
Performing Arts Library, *73*
Pershing, General "Blackjack," *35, 80*
Pershing Park, *35*
Petersen House, *57*
Pharmacies, *xvi*
Phillips Collection, *68–69, 125*
Phillips Flagship ✕, *95*
Phoenix (shop), *147*
Phoenix Park Hotel, *107–108*
Pizzeria Paradiso ✕, *101*
Pop clubs, *134*
Pope, John Russell, *69*
Potomac Spirit, *xviii–xix*
Presidents, *5–6*
Primi Piatti ✕, *99*

R

Ramsay, William, *79*
Ramsay House, *79*
Records, *148–149*
Red Room, White House, *38*
Red Sage ✕, *100*
Renwick, James, *35*
Renwick Gallery, *35–36*
Restaurants, *17, 18, 31, 33, 37, 44, 46, 49, 86–99, 92–105*
African, *89*
American, *94, 96, 102–103*
Asian, *96–97*
Caribbean, *103, 105*
Chinese, *100–101*
Ethiopian, *89, 92*
French, *92, 95, 97–98, 103–104*
Indian, *98–99, 104*
Indonesian, *104*
International, *105*
Italian, *92, 101*
Malaysian, *92*
Mediterranean, *93*
Middle Eastern, *93, 101*
Moroccan, *99*
New American, *93, 102, 104–105*
Seafood, *95*
South American, *119*
Southern, *95, 99–100*
Southwestern/Tex-Mex, *100*
Spanish, *100*
Thai, *102*
Trinidadian, *93–94*
Vietnamese, *94*
Retrospective (shop), *144*
Rhythm and blues clubs, *134*
Ritz (club), *132*
Ritz-Carlton ⊡, *114*
River Club ✕, *104–105, 132–133*
River Inn ⊡, *119*
Rizik Bros. (shop), *150*
Robert A. Taft Memorial, *46–47*
Rock clubs, *134*
Roosevelt, Theodore, *20*

S

Saigon Gourmet ✕, *94*
St. John's Episcopal Church, *36*
Sak's Fifth Avenue (department store), *140, 143*
Sala Thai ✕, *102*

Sarinah Satay House ✕, *104*
Sasakawa Peace Foundation, *84*
Scruggs, Jan, *27*
Sculpture Garden, *16*
Seasons, *xxvii–xxviii*
Second Story Books (shop), *145*
Senate, *43–44*
Senate chambers, *44*
Senior citizens, hints for, *xvii–xviii, xxvi*
Serenade Record Shop, *149*
Sewall-Belmont House, *47–48*
Shakespeare Theatre, *127*
Sharper Image (shop), *140*
Shear Madness (show), *122*
Shoes, *149*
Shoe Scene (shop), *149*
Sholl's Colonial Cafeteria ✕, *96*
Shopping, *136–137, 140, 142–150*
antiques and collectibles, *143–144*
books, *144–145*
children's clothing and toys, *145–146*
clothing, men's, *148*
clothing, women's, *148, 149–150*
crafts and gifts, *146–147*
department stores, *142–143*
jewelry, *147*
leather goods, *147*
records, *148–149*
shoes, *149*
shopping districts, *136–137, 140, 142*
specialty stores, *143–150*
The Shops at National Place (mall), *140*
Sign of the Whale (bar), *130*
Skewers ✕, *101*
Skynear and Company (shop), *147*
Smithson, James, *21*
Smithsonian Associates Program, *122*
Smithsonian Information Center, *21*
Smithsonian Institution, *124*
Smithsonian Institution Building, *21*
Source Theatre, *127–128*
Spirit of Washington, xviii
Stabler-Leadbeater Apothecary, *79*
State Dining Room, White House, *39*
Statuary Hall, *43*
Steilmann European Selection (shop), *137*
Straits of Malaya ✕, *92*
Stouffer Renaissance Mayflower ⊡, *112*

Studio Theatre, *128*
Subway, *xiv, xix–xx, xxvii*
Summer Opera Theater Company, *126*
Supreme Court Building, *48*
Susquehanna (shop), *144*
Suter's Tavern, plaque for, *63*
Sylvan Theater, *126*

T

Tabard Inn ✕, *102*
Taberna del Alabardero ✕, *100*
Taft, Robert A., *46–47*
Taft, William Howard, *48, 80*
Takoma Station Tavern (jazz club), *134*
Taxis, *xiv, xx, xxvii*
Telephones, *xxvii*
Terrace Theater, *121*
Textile Museum, *69–70*
Theater, *127–128*
Theater Lab, *121*
Thornton, William, *34, 40, 63*
Thurgood Marshall Federal Judiciary Building, *48*
Tickets, *122*
Tidal Basin, *26*
  paddleboats on, *26*
Tiffany, Louis, *29*
Timing the trip, *xxvii–xxviii*
Tomb of the Unknown Soldier of the American Revolution, *79*
TomTom ✕, *93*
Torpedo Factory Arts Center, *79–80*
Tourist information, *xx*
Tours, *xviii–xix*
  boat, *xviii–xix*
  bus, *xviii, xix*
  orientation, *xviii*
  special-interest, *xix*
  walking, *xix*
Tower Records (shop), *149*
Tracks (dance club), *133*
Trains, *xiv, xx*
Transportation, *xiii–xv*
  by bus, *xiii, xiv–xv, xxi–xxii*
  by car, *xiv, xv, xxiv*
  by plane, *xiii, xxi*
  by subway, *xiv*
  by taxi, *xiv*
  by train, *xiv*
Treasury Building, *36–37*

Treaty of Ghent, *34*
Trover Books (shop), *145*
Truman, Harry, *37*
Tudor Place, *63–64*
Two Quail ✕, *94*

U

U Street, *87–88, 105*
Uniform (shop), *144*
Union Station, *xiv, 48–49, 142*
United States Botanic Gardens, *49*
United States Holocaust Memorial Museum, *22*
Upper Connecticut Avenue, hotels on, *117–118*

V

Van Buren, Martin, *31*
Vaux, Calvert, *40*
Vertigo Books, *145*
Victoria's Secret (shop), *140*
Vietnam Veterans Memorial, *26–27*
Vietnam Women's Memorial, *27*
Vincenzo al Sole ✕, *101*
Visas, *xvii, xxvi*
Visitor information, *xx*

W

Walker Collection, *29*
Warner Theatre, *127*
Washington, George, *28, 40, 42, 43, 56, 63, 77, 78, 79*
Washington, Martha, *43*
Washington Ballet, *122*
Washington Courtyard by Marriott ▥, *115*
Washington, D.C., Convention and Visitors Association, *xx*
Washington Dolls' House and Toy Museum, *84*
Washington Hilton and Towers, *115*
Washington Monument, *27–28*
Washington National Cathedral, *125*
Washington Opera, *126–127*
Washington Stage Guild, *128*
Watergate Hotel, *74, 118–119*
Weather, *xxvii–xxviii*
West End
  hotels in, *118–119*
  restaurants in, *87, 102–105*

White House, *28, 37–39*
Blue Room, 38
East Room, 38
Green Room, 38
Oval Office, 38
Red Room, 38
State Dining Room, 39
tickets, 39
visitor center, 39
Williams-Sonoma (shop), *140*
William Tecumseh Sherman Monument, *39*
Wood, Waddy, *32*

Woodrow Wilson House, *70*
Woolly Mammoth (theater company), *128*

Y

Yawa (bookstore), *145*

Z

Zed Restaurant (country club), *129*
Zei (dance club), *133*
Zoos
National Zoological Park, 82–83

NOTES

NOTES

Fodor's Travel Publications

Available at bookstores everywhere, or call 1–800–533–6478, 24 hours a day.

Gold Guides
U.S.

Alaska

Arizona

Boston

California

Cape Cod, Martha's Vineyard, Nantucket

The Carolinas & the Georgia Coast

Chicago

Colorado

Florida

Hawai'i

Las Vegas, Reno, Tahoe

Los Angeles

Maine, Vermont, New Hampshire

Maui & Lana'i

Miami & the Keys

New England

New Orleans

New York City

Pacific North Coast

Philadelphia & the Pennsylvania Dutch Country

The Rockies

San Diego

San Francisco

Santa Fe, Taos, Albuquerque

Seattle & Vancouver

The South

U.S. & British Virgin Islands

USA

Virginia & Maryland

Washington, D.C.

Foreign

Australia

Austria

The Bahamas

Belize & Guatemala

Bermuda

Canada

Cancún, Cozumel, Yucatán Peninsula

Caribbean

China

Costa Rica

Cuba

The Czech Republic & Slovakia

Eastern & Central Europe

Europe

Florence, Tuscany & Umbria

France

Germany

Great Britain

Greece

Hong Kong

India

Ireland

Israel

Italy

Japan

London

Madrid & Barcelona

Mexico

Montréal & Québec City

Moscow, St. Petersburg, Kiev

The Netherlands, Belgium & Luxembourg

New Zealand

Norway

Nova Scotia, New Brunswick, Prince Edward Island

Paris

Portugal

Provence & the Riviera

Scandinavia

Scotland

Singapore

South Africa

South America

Southeast Asia

Spain

Sweden

Switzerland

Thailand

Tokyo

Toronto

Turkey

Vienna & the Danube

Fodor's Special-Interest Guides

Caribbean Ports of Call

The Complete Guide to America's National Parks

Family Adventures

Fodor's Gay Guide to the USA

Halliday's New England Food Explorer

Halliday's New Orleans Food Explorer

Healthy Escapes

Kodak Guide to Shooting Great Travel Pictures

Net Travel

Nights to Imagine

Rock & Roll Traveler USA

Sunday in New York

Sunday in San Francisco

Walt Disney World for Adults

Walt Disney World, Universal Studios and Orlando

Where Should We Take the Kids? California

Where Should We Take the Kids? Northeast

Worldwide Cruises and Ports of Call

Special Series

Affordables
Caribbean
Europe
Florida
France
Germany
Great Britain
Italy
London
Paris

Bed & Breakfasts and Country Inns
America
California
The Mid-Atlantic
New England
The Pacific Northwest
The South
The Southwest
The Upper Great Lakes

Berkeley Guides
California
Central America
Eastern Europe
Europe
France
Germany & Austria
Great Britain & Ireland
Italy
London
Mexico
New York City
Pacific Northwest & Alaska
Paris
San Francisco

Compass American Guides
Arizona
Canada
Chicago
Colorado
Hawaii
Idaho
Hollywood
Las Vegas
Maine
Manhattan
Montana

New Mexico
New Orleans
Oregon
San Francisco
Santa Fe
South Carolina
South Dakota
Southwest
Texas
Utah
Virginia
Washington
Wine Country
Wisconsin
Wyoming

Citypacks
Atlanta
Berline
Chicago
Hong Kong
London
Los Angeles
Montréal
New York City
Paris
Prague
Rome
San Francisco
Tokyo
Washington, D.C.

Fodor's Español
California
Caribe Occidental
Caribe Oriental
Gran Bretaña
Londres
Mexico
Nueva York
Paris

Exploring Guides
Australia
Boston & New England
Britain
California
Canada
Caribbean
China
Costa Rica
Egypt
Florence & Tuscany

Florida
France
Germany
Greek Islands
Hawai'i
Ireland
Israel
Italy
Japan
London
Mexico
Moscow & St. Petersburg
New York City
Paris
Prague
Provence
Rome
San Francisco
Scotland
Singapore & Malaysia
South Africa
Spain
Thailand
Turkey
Venice

Fodor's Flashmaps
Boston
New York
San Francisco
Washington, D.C.

Pocket Guides
Acapulco
Atlanta
Barbados
Jamaica
London
New York City
Paris
Prague
Puerto Rico
Rome
San Francisco
Washington, D.C.

Mobil Travel Guides
America's Best Hotels & Restaurants
California & the West

Frequent Traveler's Guide to Major Cities
Great Lakes
Mid-Atlantic
Northeast
Northwest & Great Plains
Southeast
Southwest & South Central

Rivages Guides
Bed and Breakfasts of Character and Charm in France
Hotels and Country Inns of Character and Charm in France
Hotels and Country Inns of Character and Charm in Italy
Hotels and Country Inns of Character and Charm in Paris
Hotels and Country Inns of Character and Charm in Portugal
Hotels and Country Inns of Character and Charm in Spain

Short Escapes
Britain
France
New England
Near New York City

Fodor's Sports
Golf Digest's Places to Play
Skiing USA
USA Today The Complete Four Sport Stadium Guide

Fodor's Vacation Planners
Great American Learning Vacations
Great American Sports & Adventure Vacations
Great American Vacations
Great American Vacations for Travelers with Disabilities
National Parks and Seashores of the East
National Parks of the West

WHEREVER YOU TRAVEL, *H*ELP IS NEVER FAR AWAY.

From planning your trip to providing travel assistance along the way, American Express® Travel Service Offices are always there to help.

Washington, D.C.

American Express Travel Service
1150 Connecticut Avenue N.W.
202/457-1300

American Express Travel Service
Mazza Gallerie, 5300 Wisconsin
3rd Floor, N.W.
202/362-4000

Travel